Mastering Engagement for Coaching Success

The Coach's Guide to Fully Invested and Motivated Coachees

Debbie Inglis

Mastering Engagement for Coaching Success:
The Coach's Guide to Fully Invested and
Motivated Coachees
©2024 Debbie Inglis

ISBN: 9781068791802 Paperback

Published by: Inspired By Publishing

The strategies in this book are presented primarily for enjoyment and educational purposes. Every effort has been made to trace copyright holders and obtain their permission for the use of copyright material.

The information and resources provided in this book are based upon the authors' personal experiences. Any outcome, income statements or other results, are based on the authors' experiences and there is no guarantee that your experience will be the same. There is an inherent risk in any business enterprise or activity and there is no guarantee that you will have similar results as the author as a result of reading this book.

The author reserves the right to make changes and assumes no responsibility or liability whatsoever on behalf of any purchaser or reader of these materials.

Dedication

For Mum and Dad,

Thanks for your unwavering support and belief in me.

Mum, your strength and courage has been the cornerstone in much of what I do–including helping me to get this book finished!

Dad, thanks for your creative inspiration, positivity and sense of humour! I miss you loads, and I'm saddened that you're not here to see this book completed.

All my love to you both.

xx

Acknowledgements

I'm grateful to have been influenced by so many people during my development as a coach, all of whom have contributed in some way to the experiences I share in this book.

To Lyn Priestley, for pointing me towards coaching when I was at a crossroads, and to Kim Morgan and Louise Trevatt for showing me how it's done!

To all the coaches and supervisors who've held me accountable, challenged my thinking and championed my growth, including Claire Cahill, Nicky Davies, Carole Whyley and Sarah Wray.

To those who've helped by sharing their experiences during my research, specifically Andrew Blench, Kat Brown, Susan Graves, Rosey Moloney, Rebecca Norton, Alison Steele and Helen Webb. Thanks too, to Ruth Town for your helpful feedback on the early draft of this book.

Thank you to graphic designer Sarah Hepburn for your timely and professional production of the graphics for this book.

Thanks to all the cafés I've spent time in whilst putting pen to paper. I believe I've bought my fair share of teas, coffees and cakes!

Special thanks to all at Inspired By Publishing for your amazing support, helpful accountability and feedback, and for keeping me motivated.

And finally, thanks to all the coaches I've trained and those in my Supervision Plus Membership Group, for putting your faith in me to be part of your coaching development.

Contents

Introduction

What makes you feel most fulfilled as a coach? Perhaps it's when a client gives you great feedback or a glowing testimonial. Maybe, it's seeing the changes or transformations in your coachees. Or, could it be you're at your most fulfilled when you find yourself fully booked with clients?

Whatever your reasons, coaching is often most successful when the coachee is prepared and highly invested in their development. The sessions flow, supported by a good level of rapport, and coachees see moments of "stuckness" as opportunities for learning.

As I celebrate 20 years as a coach, I think fondly of the people I've worked with, the journeys they've been on and the transformations they've achieved. It's such a rewarding role, and I love the fact that it's about empowering people. But in order for both you and your coachees to get the most out of coaching, I believe that you need to master *engagement*.

Let's start by getting clear on what I mean by "coaching," as there are mixed messages around what it is.

When I talk about coaching in this book, I'm referring to the partnership between coach and coachee, and the safe environment which the coach creates to enable supportive challenge that helps the coachee progress towards desired outcomes.

It involves a unique combination of mindset and skills, enhanced by a range of tools, all of which make for a creative, thought-provoking and developmental experience between the coach and coachee.

It's not making judgements about a coachee's actions or behaviours, or about telling the coachee what to do. Neither is it about the coach sharing the benefit of their knowledge and experience in the hope the coachee adopts their ideas. It's about our belief that the coachee has the answers within them, or the resources to find them.

Over my years of running coach-training courses, I've met so many people who believe that they already have experience in coaching others, only to realise that their assumption of what coaching entails was incorrect.

Most of the time, they realise they've been *mentoring*, as their support has involved giving advice and sharing the benefits of their experience in the hope it will be followed, or at least tried.

There's a place for mentoring, and there's also a place for coaching. We need to be clear about the difference between the two through our messaging and during our pre-coaching conversations, so that our clients and coachees fully understand their role in the process and what they're buying into.

In order to become a successful *coach*, engagement is key; it's a necessary and crucial part of coaching success. I'd argue that it's even more important now, given our fast-paced lives, the potential for superficial attention and the depth of thoughts we need to employ to achieve great results.

When you think about engagement in coaching, who do you think it involves?

I have often found that many coaches focus a lot on the coachee's engagement but forget to also factor in their own!

Engagement in coaching starts well before the actual sessions even begin. It is about purposeful involvement at *all* stages of the coaching process, and covers:

- How we get the coachee's buy-in from the start and facilitate their continued engagement throughout the process
- How we manage or even eliminate factors that can negatively impact engagement – both the coachee's and our own
- How we ensure successful coaching conclusions and engagement in continued learning and development
- How we maintain and enhance our own engagement, staying motivated and confident in our abilities
- How we build engagement with new clients, so we can have a bigger impact in the areas that we're passionate about and want to make a difference in

Although we may feel that once the coachee starts their coaching journey with us, it's their responsibility to remain invested. After all, they're responsible for their goals and actions, for arriving on time and for owning their progress (or even lack of).

But I believe we have lots of opportunities to influence the coachee's engagement, maintain or boost their motivation and tap into their learning styles and so on, in order to facilitate the best outcomes for them. We also need to be mindful of our own impact on the engagement process and where we may unwittingly sabotage this.

The aim of this book is to explore how we maximise all opportunities for engagement, to ensure the best results for the coachee *and* for ourselves.

To this end, I've created the 4-part Coaching Engagement Model™, which permeates all aspects of a coaching relationship, even before you and the coachee meet.

The 4-part Coaching Engagement Model™

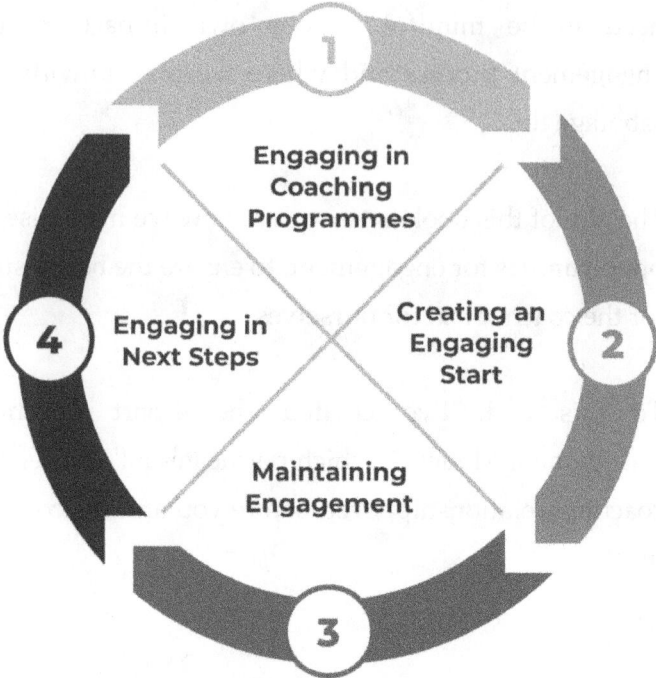

Part 1: Engaging in Coaching Programmes

The model starts with a focus on what I believe are the three most important ingredients to set up effective engagement before coaching actually starts:

1. The message we put out to attract coachees
2. The pre-coaching conversation and what is most important to include

3. The contracting process, both formal and informal, detailing how you'll work together and tips for making the most of the sessions

Part 2: Creating an Engaging Start

The second part is all about good preparation and ways in which we can create a clear and confident start to each coaching session. It starts with a range of activities and strategies for preparation, including ideas for the coachee. Then, it moves on to three options for session introductions, including resource ideas.

Part 3: Maintaining Engagement

Once coaching gets underway, we need to maintain engagement and investment. Despite our best intentions, things *can* get in the way, including ourselves. This section looks at how we, as coaches, can disrupt engagement, reducing the potential for coachee success. I follow this with a chapter on what causes a coachee to get "stuck," when we should embrace this and how we can best respond.

Part 4: Engaging in Next Steps

In the final part of this book, I share ideas for creating a strong finish both to individual sessions and coaching programmes, and why this is important for the coachee's ongoing development. And lastly, I turn the focus back on you as the coach, sharing creative ways to reflect on your practice, so that you continue to learn and grow, engaging new coachees and starting the engagement cycle again, but with more knowledge, skills and experience.

When sitting down to write this book, I was motivated by the knowledge that I have lots of ideas and resources to share with new and developing coaches, as well as those who are keen to improve engagement within their coaching programmes. As a result, this book is more practical than theoretical.

Within each of the four parts, you'll find lots of practical ideas that you can use and benefit from straight away, including questions, models and resources for boosting engagement. You'll also gain confidence from having an extended toolkit to draw upon, and I hope these ideas will provide inspiration for you to create your own tools as well.

Over the years, via my coaching training and supervision, I've seen coaches succumb to self-doubt and low confidence due to a coachee's lack of engagement, unsure what went wrong and what to do about it. This book aims to address this. To start, it's helpful to recognise the signs of when a coachee is engaged versus when they *aren't* engaged.

When coachees are engaged:

- They're invested in their development; they're willing to play their part and take responsibility for their goals and actions.
- They can see the benefits of coaching and arrive for each session with anticipation of what gems they will come away with, whether that's new solutions or new self-knowledge.
- Sessions flow and have a clear purpose, ranging from having some space to work through thoughts and ideas to a very specific issue that needs a solution.
- And they enjoy the process (as do you!).

When coachees aren't engaged:

- They miss out on the opportunity to grow professionally and personally in a forum where they can be fully open and honest without fear of judgement.
- Their lack of "buy-in" could result in them seeing coaching as "no good" or "not for them", even discounting it as a potential developmental option for others, such as team members who are struggling or are keen to achieve their full potential and are seeking support.

- They (or their organisation) are spending money on a service that is having little or no impact, so it's seen as a waste of time and money.
- Worst case scenario, they could attribute this waste of money to *you* specifically, which impacts your reputation, credibility and potential referral opportunities.

What other signs have you spotted that tell you your coachees are engaged or not?

Clarity from the outset will help ensure appropriate engagement, and the sooner the coachee is engaged, the more likely they are to make progress and see results. This provides greater scope for success, which leads to more repeat business and referrals.

I believe that coaching has the power to transform the lives of *willing* coachees. As coaches, we can optimise this willingness to engage, by taking advantage of the range of opportunities throughout the coaching process that are open to us. This book explores those opportunities.

Part 1: Engaging in Coaching Programmes

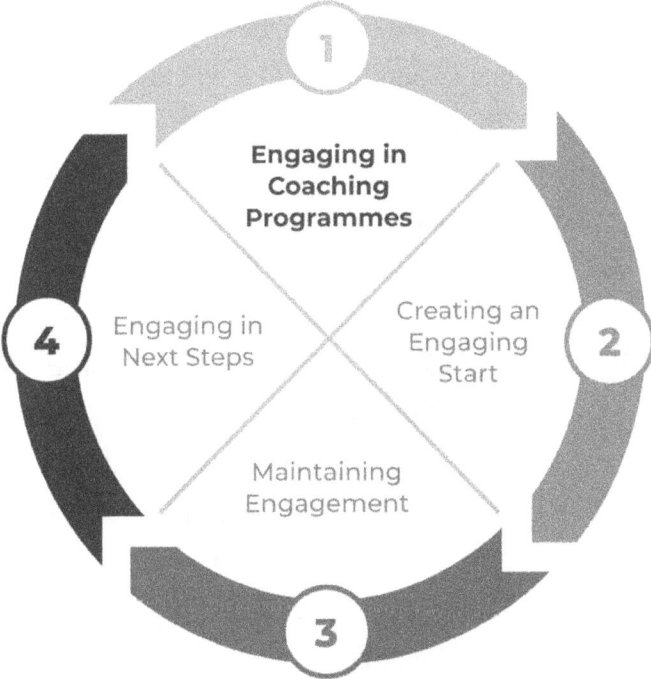

Engaging in Coaching Programmes

1

Creating an Engaging Start

2

Maintaining Engagement

3

Engaging in Next Steps

4

Imagine the scenario…

One of your coachees arrives for their third session and, following the initial greetings and sit-down, they seem a little uncomfortable. You ask how they are feeling about today's session and, after a pause, they reply, "OK," shifting in their chair as they speak, leading you to be unconvinced by their response.

Reviewing the coaching relationship to date, the coachee seemed happy to explore coaching as part of their professional development when you had the pre-coaching meeting. They were curious about how it could help them.

In their first coaching session, they took a while to open up. You listened well, asked open questions and used your rapport-building skills to help put them at ease. As this session progressed, you noticed the coachee visibly relax and start providing longer answers. The session ended with the coachee identifying something they could work on linked to their goal, and you agreed on a date and time for the second session.

At the start of that second session, the coachee shared how they hadn't had time to complete their task, citing their workload as the reason. The session continued in a similar way to the first, with the coachee opening up after a slightly faltering start, concluding with another action set by the coachee, which they seemed confident they'd achieve.

Then at the start of this third session, there was a similar response to the start of session two, when you enquired about completion of their task and other progress.

Noticing a possible pattern developing here, you start to wonder about the coachee's level of engagement in the process, and what else might be going on for them.

Does this sound familiar? If you were the coach in this scenario, how would you be feeling at this point?

There could be a number of reasons why this coachee had not completed their task from session two. These reasons could include:

- The task could have involved someone else, who was off work on sick leave, or had been given another role, or had left the organisation.
- The coachee genuinely wanted to make changes

and understood that this involved trying out new ideas, but had not felt ready to share the main obstacle that had got in the way of making the changes on their own.

- Or they could be "going through the motions" of identifying a task, but their heart is just not in it. They're not really motivated and are attending the sessions because they have been told it will be helpful to their career.

When coachees are engaged in coaching, they are there because they *want* to be there. They've bought into the process and its benefits, and have accepted that they may have to make changes to achieve their goal. This is crucial to the process.

When coachees aren't engaged from the start, they don't fully play their part. Their effort to ensure the process is successful is reduced, you gain less information from them and it all feels very superficial.

However, not all reasons for a coachee's inaction will be due to them being disengaged from the coaching process. A good coach can address these when they spot them, or help prevent these situations by:

- Checking if the task was in the coachee's control; if it involved someone else, then discussing the alternative actions if that person was unavailable.

- Ensuring the coachee has been given opportunities in the coaching session to explore all potential obstacles and their solutions.

Of course, building rapport with the coachee from the outset will help develop trust, leading to the coachee being more open to answering challenging questions, such as those which explore obstacles to goal achievement.

But how could you avoid this situation in the first place?

From my own experience, and that of supervising other coaches, it is not uncommon for issues that occur within a coaching session to stem from what happened or did not happen before the coaching programme even began. For example:

- A coachee telling the coach that they have had coaching before, and that they know what to expect. As the first session progresses, it becomes apparent that the coachee has had mentoring previously, not coaching.
- There has been a lack of time to have a productive discussion with the coachee, particularly when coaching in an organisation,

and the coachee was offered coaching but without much knowledge of what to expect.

The core work in a coaching relationship starts before you actually start coaching.

I believe the potential for engagement starts *before* the coaching actually begins and can be split into three areas:

1. The coaching message
2. The pre-coaching conversation
3. The contracting process

In the first chapter, we will dive into each of the three areas in detail, providing practical examples you can adopt into your practice.

Chapter 1
Creating Clear Expectations

In order to maximise engagement from the start, and avoid issues arising from confused messaging, misunderstandings and assumptions, there needs to be clear communication and good management of expectations before coaching commences.

This can happen through:

- Having a clear coaching message, which attracts willing coachees.
- Having a purposeful pre-coaching conversation where the goal area is discussed, information about coaching is shared and questions are confidently answered.
- Planning how you will work together, to ensure the best outcomes.

1. The Coaching Message

This is where you create initial interest in the coaching process, and happens before the coach and coachee even meet!

The coaching message is relevant whether you are an independent coach who works with private individuals or organisations, or someone who works for an organisation and is trained in coaching skills to coach colleagues within the organisation. Ask yourself, "As a coach, what kind of message do you share to engage potential clients or coachees?"

The best marketing message will resonate with your target audience. It will speak to their situation and the solution they are seeking.

The best structure for this that I've found is:

- Who you help (briefly describe them)
- What you help them to do
- What outcomes or transformations do you help them achieve

Here are some examples:

"I help **burnt out project managers** to **identify**

strategies for avoiding overwhelm, so they **feel more in control** of their daily tasks, and **leave work with energy to spare.**"

"I help **owners of creative businesses** to **get super organised** with their ideas, so they have **a clear focus** and **get things done**, rather than being paralysed by too many ideas."

"I work with **women in the corporate sector** who want to **feel more confident in their role**, so they can **achieve their potential** and **get their dream job**."

Remember, your message isn't set in stone, so if you don't yet have enough experience of the kind of results you help your coachees achieve, start with a topic you're passionate about (e.g. confidence) or a sector you want to work with (e.g. health professionals). Then use your knowledge of this area, plus your network of contacts to identify potential issues and solutions, and speak to these in your messaging.

When I left teaching from being burnt out, I wanted to put distance between myself and that sector, even though it was the one I knew most about. It had too many negative associations. Then, through keeping in touch with some of my school contacts, I heard familiar stories of overwhelm and the issue of having no one to talk to about their problems who wouldn't repeat them to anyone else.

Coaching wasn't that well known in the education sector 20 years ago, and I suddenly realised it was my opportunity to do something positive, and be the person I had needed during *my* leadership journey in schools. Plus, some time had passed by then and I had new skills I wanted to use with people who would value my service.

My message has had several iterations over the years, with one of my favourites being:

"I help **stressed-out school leaders** create **empowered, confident and solution-focused teams**, so they can **avoid leaving a profession they love from burnout**."

Other methods for getting your message across include:

- Case studies presented as some sort of narrative or story, as in the Hero's Journey
- A series of bullet points sharing the benefits of working with you and examples of outcomes you have helped clients achieve
- A range of testimonials from previous clients

If you are an independent coach who markets your

services, your marketing message could be shared:

- On social media
- On your website
- In a webinar, workshop or talk
- Through some form of advertising, including paid adverts and sending brochures or flyers via post or email
- In a podcast or radio and television interviews, or by video

Regardless of the layout or presentation of the message, your coaching message becomes the first point of contact and first stage of engagement between you and the potential client or coachee. If it resonates with them, they'll want to know more. And the more the message resonates, the stronger the level of initial engagement between coach and coachee before the coaching even begins.

For internal coaches who work within an organisation, the message to gain a coachee's buy-in to the process is just as important, if not more so. They need to trust the process and intention behind it, including how confidentiality will be maintained.

My experience of supervising coaches who coach within the organisations they work for has highlighted ways in which the coaching offer can be "sold" to the wider staff team. This includes:

- Running a workshop where coaching is explained and some of the topics for coaching are shared
- Doing live coaching demonstrations so staff can experience how it is different from mentoring, counselling or training
- Sending out information about what coaching is and its benefits for professional and personal development

Of course the proof of the pudding is in the eating, as the saying goes, and it can take a little while for employees to engage. Starting with willing volunteers is a good first step. When these volunteers experience success, they become your "sales team", engaging more staff members to try it out, and the impact spreads.

The best marketing message will resonate with your target audience

2. The Pre-coaching Conversation

If a potential coachee has not experienced coaching before, they may exhibit a range of emotions – from happy curiosity to scepticism – so the pre-coaching conversation is crucial in making the most of the time spent in the coaching sessions. Sometimes referred to as "Discovery Calls/Conversations" or "Chemistry Sessions", a pre-coaching conversation is often the first conversation you have with a coachee.

This conversation is the perfect opportunity to start using your listening and questioning skills and building rapport, while you gain some background information and find out how invested the coachee is in the process.

Sample Pre-coaching Conversation Format

1. Discover what the coachee wants to gain from coaching, and find out about their potential goal area. Consider asking the following questions:

- What's brought them to coaching?
- What's most important to them about this?
- What outcome are they looking for?
- How soon do they want a solution?
- What do they know about coaching and how it works?

This will provide useful information about their reasons for engaging in coaching and their understanding of it, providing opportunities for you to correct any misconceptions.

2. Give them the opportunity to ask questions. In my experience, coachees have asked:

- How often do we meet?
- What experience do you have of working with someone in a similar situation as me?
- Do you offer phone/online coaching as well as in-person?
- Do you have any case studies you can share?
- How much is it?

Think of all the questions you may be asked and how you might respond.

Don't be tempted to go into, "Coaching is great! Here's why..." or go into detail about all the features and benefits of working with you if they haven't asked for this information. Have you ever done this and watched as the person you are talking to has started to glaze over? I have. I can sense the point where I've lost them.

Ask them what questions they have and answer each one with clarity and certainty. Once you have answered one question, ask what other questions they have. Repeat until they have no more questions.

Be sure of yourself and your answers so that the coachee can start building their trust in you, and their belief that you can help them find the outcome they're looking for. This will increase their buy-in and engagement from the start.

3. Identify next steps. If they are ready to start working with you, progress to your next step. This may include sending them a summary of what you've discussed, your coaching agreement or contract and arranging your first coaching session.

You will also need to identify a time to have your "informal contracting" conversation, which could be a separate conversation before your first coaching session, or added to the start of this coaching session. See the next section for more on informal contracting.

If they are unsure about progressing further at this stage and want some time to think about it, agree on a time when you will contact them again to follow up.

Pre-coaching Conversations in Organisations

If you are an independent coach who is going into an organisation to coach one or more of the staff members, it is vital to have an initial meeting with a stakeholder, such as the coachee's line manager, to find out what the organisation's expectations are from the coaching process. Your questions here might include:

- What outcomes are you looking to achieve from this coaching programme?
- How will you know it has been successful? How will you measure success?

You also need to manage the stakeholder's expectations, emphasising that the content of the coaching sessions is confidential. In addition, you need to agree on what feedback will be shared or kept confidential during and at the end of the programme of coaching sessions.

The most successful coaching programmes that I have experienced have included a three-way conversation involving the coachee, their line manager or relevant stakeholder and myself. This created an open and transparent approach where everyone understood their role in the process and the coachee was involved in the conversation where confidentiality is discussed. Part of this conversation was an agreement on what information would be fed back to the line manager, namely:

- The coachee's overall goal
- How many sessions were completed
- General information about follow-up actions from sessions
- The coachee's overall outcomes, including any statistical information where measurement tools were used at the start and end of the coaching programme, such as the Leadership Wheel, an adaptation of the Wheel of Life.

Use the link or scan the QR code below to view and download examples of these tools.
https://go.theleadershipcoachingacademy.com/bookresources

The more the coachee knows about how the coaching programme will work and how much or how little information will be shared, the more they will build rapport and trust in the coach, maximising engagement in the sessions and outcomes from the process.

3. The Contracting Process

This is where you plan out how you will work together. In some situations, this may happen straight after the discovery call, or immediately before a coaching session. It can be divided into a formal and an informal process.

Formal Contracting

This is usually a document that outlines the roles and responsibilities of all those involved. With private individuals purchasing coaching, the contract is signed by the coach and coachee. Where an organisation is the sponsor, the contract is usually signed by the coach and sponsor.

This contract may cover:

- Roles and responsibilities, including:
  - Coach: responsible for maintaining confidentiality and managing coaching boundaries

- Coachee: arriving on time and being prepared; identifying their goal and linked actions
- Number, frequency and duration of sessions
- Venue for coaching
- General goal area
- Your fees

Informal Contracting

This is the nuts and bolts of how you work together. It is more fluid and adaptable than the formal contract, offering the flexibility to change as the coaching programme progresses and the coachee discovers more about themselves, the coaching process and what are the best learning conditions for them.

Some of the things you could discuss include:

- How to prepare for the first session.
- How to ensure there are no interruptions–which is especially relevant when you are going to the coachee's place of work.
- How do they prefer to learn? Do they like to make notes or use paper and pens to brainstorm new ideas?
  - Some coaches give their coachees a notebook to make notes during coaching

sessions. Others suggest the coachee brings their own writing materials to the sessions. Find out what the coachee would prefer.

- What happens when the coachee gets "stuck"? How would they like you to respond?
  - If they say, "Give me some ideas," then you know you need to clarify what coaching is, and check that they are happy to continue.

With coachees who have been coached before, I also ask, "What does challenge look like for you in a coaching session?"

Challenge is what will take them out of their comfort zone, and some coachees like a high level of challenge. They are ready to embrace this, and realise they need a push. I ask them to describe this to me, and have had responses such as:

- "Don't let me get away with 'I don't know' when you ask me a question that really makes me think."
- "Don't be afraid to ask more probing questions if I seem to be avoiding something."

In my experience, exploring levels of challenge from the outset increases the coachee's investment in their own learning. Challenge is what moves the coachee forward and helps them get results. See Chapter 4 for different ways to positively challenge the coachee.

Summary

Coachee engagement from the outset is crucial for successful sessions.

When the coachee is engaged:

- They understand what is involved and expected of them.
- They have bought into the benefits and impact of coaching.
- They have embraced the idea of change and are willing to step outside of their comfort zone.

When the coachee is not engaged:

- They could feel like the coaching sessions are a waste of time, which could be better spent doing something else. (As could you!)
- They miss out on opportunities for personal and professional development.
- They don't see the full value of coaching and all its benefits, and could even discount it as a potential resource for others, based on their own limiting experiences.
- They, or their organisation, are spending money on a service that is having little or no impact, so is seen as a waste of money.

Actions

1. Create or update your marketing message and how your coaching offer is shared with potential clients.

    Does it represent what they will experience from your coaching? Is it truly authentic, so that those who resonate with this message will continue to be engaged when working with you?

2. Review your pre-coaching conversation format.

    Make sure there is sufficient time devoted to this. What assumptions are you making about the coachee's understanding of coaching? Are you being too heavy handed with sharing the features and benefits of coaching and not focusing on what specifically the coachee wants to know?

3. What does your informal contracting process look like at the moment?

    What else can you add? Ask your coachees for feedback on this process. How helpful is it? What could be improved to make the coaching process more impactful for them?

Part 2: Creating an Engaging Start

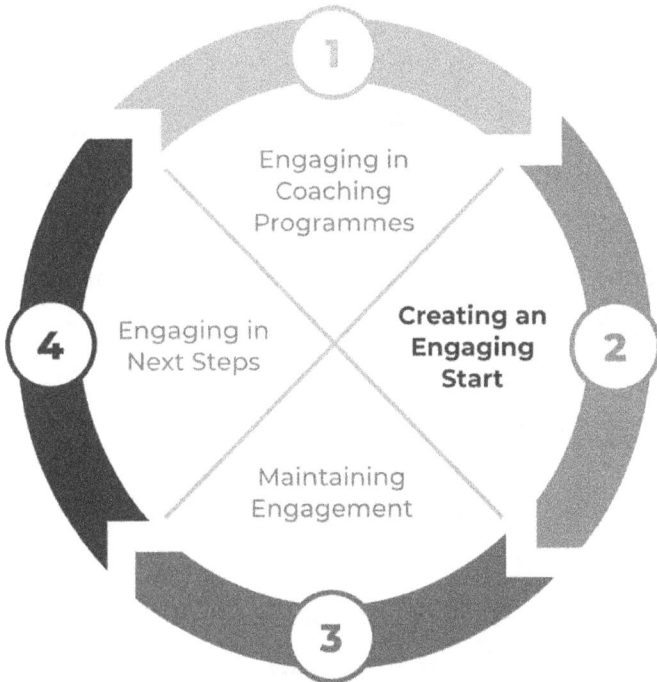

Engaging in Coaching Programmes

Engaging in Next Steps

Creating an Engaging Start

Maintaining Engagement

In our busy lives, people rarely have relaxing gaps between their daily activities. They move swiftly from one thing to another, barely taking a breath. Our technology-filled world has made it easier to be contacted, and often expectations are high for replies to be swift.

For these reasons, coachees can take longer to settle into sessions as they get into the right mindset – unless we advise them otherwise and offer strategies for a really good start.

Of course, we don't live in a perfect world, and sometimes coachees will turn up to a session unprepared, often as a result of things beyond their control. In this situation, we can use one or two preparation ideas for the first few minutes to help them settle in, giving them thinking space between their last activity and this session.

While Part 1 offered strategies for a successful start of engagement, Part 2 offers ideas to help our coachees prepare for their sessions, maximising their engagement and generating better outcomes. It also offers ideas for our own preparation, and what can happen if we're not prepared.

Chapter 2
Preparing for a Clear Start

Getting a coaching session off to a strong, purposeful and engaging start is not only about a clear beginning to each session, but also involves good preparation.

When you don't arrive prepared for a coaching session, you risk a "waffly" start, a lack of focus and direction, and the coachee losing their trust and confidence in you.

When you are *both* prepared, it makes for a more fulfilling session, and time is used productively.

The Coach

A coach who is not prepared runs the risk of playing catch-up in the session, feeling less in control of themselves.

On the other hand, a prepared coach will be more attentive to the coachee from the outset. This level of presence will ensure that they do not miss the subtleties in the coachee's communication. This might include repetition of key words or phrases, which would benefit from further exploration.

For example, you may miss the choice of, and emphasis on, certain words the coachee uses in a sentence, such as: "I'm **always** messing up my communication with this team member; I **never** get it right."

When I am paying full attention and am present, I will be curious to know more about "always" and "never", and what the evidence is for these thoughts. They suggest limiting beliefs around the coachee's communication with this team member and warrants further discussion. This could be crucial to a positive outcome and achievement of the coachee's goal.

A prepared coach is also open-minded and flexible, ready for whatever the coachee brings to the session. They are not making assumptions about the coachee's frame of mind or the progress they may or may not have made since you last met.

The Coachee

A prepared coachee knows what they want to focus on when they meet their coach. They have given themselves some time to prepare, and are ready to provide feedback about their level of progress since the previous coaching session.

A prepared coachee will be more engaged and open to learning new things about themselves, which will help them gain new insights. They will be willing to be challenged on thoughts that may be holding them back, trusting their coach to support them in this process.

New Coachees

When a coachee is new to coaching, they will need guidance on:

- What their role is
- What the coach's role is
- What they need to bring, if anything
- What to expect from a coaching session
- And how to prepare themselves to get the most from the time they have with their coach

In the next section, I will share how I help to prepare my coachees. By the end of the section, perhaps you'll have other ideas that you can add to the list.

Why is preparation so important?

Time is such a precious commodity these days, and whether you coach within an organisation or work as an independent coach, your time and the coachee's time is valuable.

When you are both prepared, it enables you to "hit the ground running" with a clear and strong start, getting into the productive flow of coaching more quickly. You are both engaged, motivated and curious about what's in store and what will come out of the session ahead. As a result, time will be well spent.

A prepared coachee is a more engaged coachee

Preparing the Coachee

Your discovery session or pre-coaching conversation is a great opportunity to share some ideas with your coachee that will help increase their readiness for and engagement in the sessions.

I like to share some practical tips at the start of the coaching programme to help coachees get the most from the sessions. These include:

- **Come with an open mind.**
  The more open they are to new possibilities, the more likely they are to achieve their targets/goals, and learn new and useful things about themselves.

- **Be prepared to be honest with yourself.**
  Honest reflection is part of having an open mind, and will require a good level of rapport between coachee and coach.

- **Be prepared to come to each session with an update on progress towards your goal since you last met.**
  This often helps to identify where the coachee wants to spend their time in that session. Sometimes I've experienced a total switch of the

goal, based on a change of circumstances, and the goal is no longer relevant. Or the coachee hasn't achieved what they wanted to in between sessions due to some obstacle that needs exploring in the upcoming session.

- **Bring something to make notes with.**
  This is completely optional of course, but if they like to make notes to use or reflect on later, that is their responsibility. It is not your responsibility as a coach to share your notes with them. This is important for a few reasons:

  Firstly, what you make notes about and how you record your thoughts could be misconstrued by the coachee and hold a different meaning for them than they have for you.

  Secondly, you may not capture the points which the coachee considers most important and meaningful to them from that session, so their key learning points may be missed.

  Thirdly, the coachee could become reliant upon you to record a summary of the session, taking away their responsibility for their own learning and capturing that learning.

Time to Prepare

Setting aside at least five minutes to prepare for each session will help them maximise the time you have together.

When working with team leaders and managers in organisations, I've found that coachees will come to the session straight from a meeting, a previous task, a tricky conversation, or anything else that's part of their day-to-day role. There's no buffer time between the two events, other than perhaps the journey time to the room where you are meeting.

This travel time is often very short, and isn't being used to prepare for the coaching, it's being used to process the conversation or event that's just happened, and perhaps think of any follow-up actions they need to take.

As a result, time is spent at the start of the coaching session with the coach helping the coachee to "clear the clutter" of what's gone before, freeing up mental space for creative thinking and learning.

This is all about helping the coachee become present, or maximise their level of engagement.

The Coaching Space

When I coach staff in an organisation, unless we've identified a neutral space, I rely on the sponsor of the programme to provide the coaching space where we'll work. Therefore, it's important to have a conversation ensuring this is a confidential space where we won't be overheard, and the coachee feels like they can talk freely.

Ideally, sessions work well when there's a window in the room, which can be opened. I've worked in a room that became quite stuffy, making it harder for the coachee to focus. As a coach, when you have a few sessions in this kind of room it can impact on your concentration and focus too. I once ended up with a migraine! A jug or bottles of water is also a good idea.

Whilst it may be useful to have a desk or table in the room, avoid having this between you both, as this can provide a sub-conscious barrier which can impact on rapport. I've also found that this type of set-up can feel like it's a meeting instead of a coaching session. The best arrangement is two comfortable chairs at a slight angle to each other (not directly facing each other), and at a comfortable distance apart. I often ask the coachee which chair they'd like to sit in for the session.

Having other chairs in the room and some space also lends itself well to different types of coaching activities, such as Perceptual Positions. Perceptual Positions is a really powerful exercise to use when a coachee would benefit from gaining greater understanding of a situation by seeing it from different viewpoints. The chairs represent the coachee, other key people involved, and an observer's viewpoint, with the coachee spending time in each position to deepen their self-awareness and increase empathy. This leads to more informed decision-making when identifying next steps.

When it's down to the coachee to sort or book the room, let them know your thoughts on a suitable coaching space. When they have control over choosing the best space, it positively impacts on their engagement in the programme.

Other spaces where coaching sessions can be held inside include hotel foyers, hotel lounge areas and coffee shops. Even though there's the potential to be overheard, I've found that the coachees are happy in that environment because no one knows them, and they feel open to talking freely.

For example, I've coached a headteacher who chose a well known brand coffee shop for our sessions, saying it feels better to have a space away from the distractions of school for coaching. This observation has been echoed by other coachees, preferring to meet somewhere they are not constrained by their everyday environment.

This observation is so true! Our thinking can be influenced, and sometimes limited, by the environments we are routinely in; environments where we habitually do the same things and the same thinking.

For example, have you ever said to yourself:

- "I think better when I'm out of the office/my house."
- "I often do my best thinking when I'm walking the dog."
- "I solve all my work-related problems on my journey home."

Which of the above resonates most with you?

What else do you say to yourself?

Coaching Walks

Staying on the topic of getting out of the working or home environment, there are benefits to exploring the option of coaching walks when you discuss the coaching programme environment with coachees.

In simple terms, a coaching walk involves having your coaching session whilst walking with your coachee, usually outdoors. I've coached in several different spaces, including woodland and moorland areas, along a beach, and in urban areas.

Just as you would match a coachee whilst sitting in one place, it's important to check in with your coachee about your walking pace; you don't want to wear them out or go too slowly! Pace can impact thinking, as can opportunities to stop and reflect on questions, often gaining inspiration from the environment.

I've had so many positive comments from coachees who've experienced this different form of coaching, although admittedly it's not for everyone.

Coaching walks have many benefits including:

- It gets coachees out of their usual environment, as discussed above.
- It gives a different view of your surroundings, which changes as you walk, and helps you become more open-minded and creative in your thinking.
- It suits coachees who can feel uncomfortable with direct eye contact, as they are looking at

their surroundings rather than feeling the need to look directly at you.

Self-Reflective Question:

How else do you prepare for the coaching programme as a whole?

Preparing Yourself

There are several ways to get yourself ready and engaged for your coaching sessions.

I've spoken with many coaches over the years about this and everyone has their own unique way of doing it, often having more than one strategy in their repertoire to draw upon. This is a good idea, as we're all human and don't show up for our coaching sessions in exactly the same way each time. It depends on what event or situation has come up just prior to the session, or what else is going on in our lives generally. There will be times where we'll need to work harder than usual to be prepared.

As such, it's a good idea to develop our own general preparation routine, using strategies that work best for us. With experience, this will become ingrained and happen more automatically. Nevertheless, I still think it's worth reviewing this from time to time (such as during supervision sessions) to ensure we don't get stale.

There are several different preparation strategies you can use as a coach to ensure you're present for and engaged in each coaching session. The section below lists a few that you could use to either create or review your preparation routine.

Get in the Right Mindset

Getting in the right mindset is about clearing your own clutter, and freeing up your thinking space for the session ahead. Ideas include:

- **Brain dump.**
  Getting any distracting thoughts out of your head and on to paper. Digital tools, such as voice notes or typing thoughts into a document or writing app, are also useful for capturing thoughts.

- **Go for a walk.**
  A change of environment is often a good way to clear your head, as discussed above. You don't have to go outside; you could walk around the building you're in.

- **Do breathing exercises.**

  More and more people are using a variety of mindfulness-type exercises to calm their thinking and bring their attention to the present. They don't have to be long. I often do one that lasts about a minute (you can use your watch or phone to time it), where I just close my eyes and focus on my breathing.

  Yes, I can get distracted. But I just briefly notice and accept the distracting thought without judging it either way, and bring my attention back to my breathing. It takes a bit of practice, but I've found it worthwhile.

  You can extend the time if you find it helpful, and focus on what's going on in the environment around you. I like to pay attention to sounds I can hear and how the room feels around me by asking myself questions such as:

  - What's the temperature like?
  - How does the ground feel under my feet?
  - How comfortable am I in this chair?

  It's all about noticing and paying attention to your surroundings, which is an extremely useful state to be in when you start working with your coachee, so that you'll better notice what's going on for them.

- **The 1 to 10 scale.**
  As you get ready for your session, ask yourself, "On a scale of 1 to 10, how present am I for this session?" If your score is less than 8, ask yourself what you need to do or think about to be more present and engaged in the time you have left before the session. Then do that!

Prepare the Environment

Creating the optimum coaching space was discussed earlier in this chapter. Sometimes you will have more flexibility with this than others, such as having a room designated for coaching, versus a quiet corner in a hotel foyer or cafe.

Wherever possible, it's important to spend some time getting the coaching space fit for purpose, as creating the right environment for coaching will increase engagement and maximise outcomes for the coachee.

If I know the coachee will be in the room before the coaching session starts, I do some form of preparation beforehand, whether that's spending a few moments in the car when I arrive at the venue, or while I'm walking to the room, noticing my environment as I walk and grounding myself along the way.

Your Preparation Routine

If you haven't got a preparation routine, consider creating one using the ideas above, or speak to other coaches and see what they do.

If you already have a routine, ask yourself:

- How often do I review it to check its impact?
- Is there anything else I could be doing to be more present and engaged?

To give you an idea of how a routine can look, my personal routine is usually:

1. Prepare the environment, where possible.
2. Connect with the space.
3. Read through any notes (more useful in between sessions when I'm coaching several people in one day).
4. Do a brain dump if I'm finding it tricky to focus.
5. Finish with a short breathing exercise.

What does your preparation look like?

Summary

- Preparation for coaching sessions is equally as important for the coachee as it is for the coach.

- When you're both prepared, it makes for a more engaged and fulfilling coaching session.

- Make sure both you and the coachee set aside time for preparation, rather than use the first part of the session to "get in the flow."

- Coaching sessions that are carried out away from the coachee's normal work or home environment allows for more creative and "possibility" thinking.

Actions

1. Review the information you share with your coachees.

   Ensure it includes how to prepare for both the coaching programme and individual sessions.

2. Create a preparation routine for yourself.

   Alternatively, review your current one and adapt if appropriate.

Chapter 3
Creating a Clear Start

Have you ever felt that you've meandered your way into a coaching session, and before you know where you are, the session is halfway through and you're not exactly sure what the coachee wants from your time together?

Imagine the scenario...

> The coachee arrives for their coaching session, sits down, and before you have a chance to say anything, they launch into an offloading of thoughts and feelings, barely stopping for breath.

> After a while, you start wondering if this is useful for them, and whether you should "intervene" with a question when they pause in their narrative.

You find yourself preoccupied with waiting for them to finish, so you can ask your question, and this lack of full attention is impacting on your ability to be totally present for them.

In this scenario, the coachee is obviously engaged in the confidential coaching space, and is taking full advantage of the great listener that you are.

It's a compliment! The coachee trusts you enough to share their fears, concerns and worries. They might also be thinking that what they have to say is valued, which keeps them engaged in the coaching space.

At the start of my coaching career, I had some coaching sessions where offloading occurred and not much else. The coachee thanked me at the end for providing the space for them to do this. But there was a part of me that wanted to know if there had been some sort of progress or insight for the coachee, and prompted me to ask at the end: "So what are you taking away from this session?"

The purpose of this question was twofold:

1. To encourage the coachee to reflect on their outpouring of thoughts and any conclusions they'd come to as a result.

2. To satisfy *my* need to ensure I'd done something useful (not that the first purpose isn't useful).

I would now say that the first purpose is usually the *only* reason I ask this question, and my ego doesn't need the validation it used to (I say usually!).

As coaches, we need to provide more than a listening space.

As my coaching practice was evolving, I knew that listening was important, but I was a little hesitant to provide the necessary structure to ensure there was some form of growth or progress. I was worried that I'd provide too much structure, which would result in adopting a more "directive" coaching style, which didn't feel natural to me.

I've since grown in confidence to know how to find the balance between listening to the coachee, facilitating their narratives and moving them forward.

"Knowing" is tricky. Sometimes it's just down to experience and instinct. But some useful questions I've since asked myself in this situation include:

- Do I feel my coachee has said all they need to say?

- Are they starting to repeat themselves?
- Are they getting stuck?

If I find myself answering "yes" to any of these questions, then it feels like a good place to speak.

My "speaking" might include a brief summary of the key things I've heard, followed by a question such as:

- "What are you concluding from sharing these thoughts?" or,
- "What's most important to you right now about this?"

Offloading can still lead to growth.

Facilitating an offloading of thoughts and feelings at the start of a coaching session can be really useful for the coachee, particularly as they may not get the opportunity to do this outside of coaching.

Through this flow of dialogue they are often clearing space for new thinking while processing their thoughts as they speak, pulling out the bits they feel are most important. This provides us with useful detail, which we can explore within the session using probing questions that help to unpack and consolidate their thoughts.

But when "offloading" happens regularly at the start of coaching sessions, without much apparent progress, we need to check in with the coachee to see how it's supporting their overall purpose or goal for coaching.

Types of progress for the coachee include:

- New thoughts or greater clarity around their goal area.
- Overcoming an obstacle and identifying a way forward.
- An insight about themselves, such as, "What's a useful motivator for this goal?"

Another example of a waffly start to a coaching session can occur when there's an initial chat between coach and coachee which goes beyond, "Hello, how are you?" It risks becoming a chat, not a coaching conversation.

An argument can be made for trusting the coachee to answer the "how are you?" question with something they need to say that's pertinent to their overall goal, or what they want to get from the current session.

But what if they don't? What if they use the first half of the session to talk about how they've been feeling, and only after that do they focus on their goal area?

To conclude this section, it's important that we have the skills and tools to hold the coaching space for our coachees to offload when necessary, which means listening, gathering information and not judging. Whilst at the same time, we need to be mindful that some form of growth or development needs to occur within the coaching session.

Self-Reflective Questions:

So how do you usually start a coaching session?

What does a clear, confident start look, feel and sound like – both for you and the coachee?

The next section offers ways to avoid the waffly starts, and ensures that the time you spend in the coaching session is maximised for the coachee's growth and development.

Creating Clear, Confident Starts

In this section I will offer three "clear start" options:

1. Contracting
2. Updates
3. Check-ins

I would recommend doing at least the first one in each session. The updates can happen from the second session onwards, and check-ins are optional but have useful benefits, which I'll share below.

1. Start with Contracting

A clear, confident start that maximises coachee engagement involves some form of contracting.

This is a more informal agreement than a written contract (see Chapter 2), and includes:

- First session: reaffirming the goal for coaching and exploring this in greater depth.
- Second and subsequent sessions: identifying smaller session-by-session outcomes.

Questions that Support Deeper Exploration of a Coachee's Goal

Once the overall focus or goal for coaching has been confirmed, it's well worth going deeper into this at the start of the first session with questions such as:

- In what ways does this goal stretch you?
- How does this goal support your ongoing personal (or professional) development?

- What will be better for you when you've achieved this goal?
- What else will achieving this goal help you accomplish?
- What are you hoping to learn about yourself from (working towards) this goal?

These questions are really useful in making sure that the overall goal is sufficiently challenging, supporting one of the key principles of coaching: growth and development.

They also help avoid the situation where a coachee doesn't see coaching as being of any value, because their goal wasn't sufficiently challenging and nothing had really changed for them by the end of the process.

As coaches, we need to help our coachees see value in this learning process.

Clear Start Question Examples

Prefaced by an acknowledgement of the coachee's progress towards their goal, the second or subsequent session might use one or more of the following questions to contract for the session ahead:

- What would you like to focus on in our session today?
- What do you want to achieve in today's session?
- What would be a good outcome for you today?
- Let's say we have a really productive session, what will have happened by the end?
- What could be different for you by the end of today's coaching session?
- What else?

"What else?" is a great follow-up question. From my experience, the first answer a coachee provides isn't always the most important one for them right then, particularly when identifying potential session outcomes. It encourages them to be more creative and use their imagination to consider what else is possible, and what's most important to achieve their goal.

Deeper Exploration in Practice

Using one of the questions above, here are two examples of how a coach might explore the resulting answer:

Example 1

Coach: "What outcome would you like to get from our session today?"

Coachee: "I'd like to feel less stressed about my workload."

Coach: "You'd like to feel less stressed about your workload. Tell me more about what this is like for you right now."

Coachee: "Just when I feel that I'm on top of things, my boss gives me another task that I just haven't got time to do unless I drop something else, or another task ends up being late."

The coach then asks questions to explore the coachee's current situation, followed by identifying possible options.

Example 2

Coach: "What outcome would you like to get from our session today?"

Coachee: "I'd like to feel less stressed about my workload."

Coach: "And let's say we have a really successful session, what will feeling 'less stressed about my workload' feel like?"

Coachee: "I'll feel more relaxed about the idea of going into work each day."

Coach: "What else?"

Coachee: "Erm... I'd like to have a response ready for my boss which doesn't sound aggressive, when she gives me another task."

Coach: "What else?"

Coachee: "...I think that's it. Those are the main things."

Coach: "So feeling more relaxed and having a response for your boss which is not aggressive. And what might that non-aggressive response look, feel or sound like?"

Coachee: "I'd feel confident, sure of what I was saying. I'd come across as polite and professional."

Coach:	"I'm getting a clearer sense of how you'll be next time you speak to your boss when they give you another task. What's talking through this feeling of being less stressed about your workload giving you right now?"
Coachee:	"It feels better already. I've got a better sense of what I need to work on today."
Coach:	"Great! So given what you've said… where would be a good place to start?"

As you can see from the second example that goes into greater depth when contracting on the session goal, this can provide more detail and a greater connection with the end result. It also has the potential to create progress for the coachee from the outset.

What if the coachee doesn't know what they want to get from a coaching session?

I've come across this a few times, and it can happen for a few reasons, including:

- They are stuck or confused about where to go next. Perhaps things haven't gone as they'd hoped since their last session with you. Or perhaps they have come across an obstacle and don't know how to overcome it, or what's now possible because they can't see a way past it.

- They have booked a block of coaching sessions over a period of months and, after making good progress in previous sessions, they can't think of anything else they need from the coaching process.

For the first scenario, you could respond with any of the following:

- "Given that you're feeling stuck*, what would be a good use of our time today?"
- "How might today's conversation help you become unstuck?"
- "Tell me more about 'stuck.'" (This is a useful prompt if the coachee hasn't elaborated on what being "stuck" is about.)

*Make sure you use the coachee's descriptive language about their current state, rather than reword or interpret it in your own way. How you phrase their state could have a very *different meaning for them, and you risk losing rapport if you do this.*

For the second scenario, if there's a larger or overall goal that they are working towards, this is a good opportunity to review how they're progressing towards it. This helps put their progress into perspective and see what would be a useful next step for that day's coaching session.

You could also offer them an "exit session" (see more on this in Part 4, Chapter 6), and "bank" any remaining sessions to be used within a set time period. I've offered anywhere from 6 to 12 months with clients before, but you need a time limit on this offer, especially as your fees are likely to increase beyond 12 months.

The other alternative is to cancel the coaching programme. I don't know any coaches who have offered part refunds for helping their coachees achieve their goals early. My best recommendations here are therefore:

- To offer fewer sessions in your package with the option to review and extend the programme if needed, or
- Make it clear in your pre-coaching conversation that if they achieve their goal before they use up

all their sessions, they can "bank" the remaining sessions to use within a given timeframe.

Ensuring that the Outcome is the Coachee's and not the Coach's

I've come across coachees whose goal is what they think I would like to hear, or what they feel is a good outcome to have. These are usually people who have not experienced coaching before and don't fully understand their role in the process, or it's early in the process and we haven't built enough rapport yet.

Whatever the reason, it's a good idea for the coach to maintain flexibility during the session, ready to change direction, if appropriate, for the coachee, and create a more suitable goal.

To summarise this section, a clear start is that point where both coach and coachee know *this is the coaching session*. They've stopped talking about the weather, their journey, etc. and their coach-coachee roles kick in.

Whenever I've been coached, I feel my brain changing gears when we start the coaching session. I know what to expect, and I engage the part of my brain that is open to new thinking and new possibilities. I am ready to be challenged, and consider different ways forward. I am ready to increase my self-awareness.

This is how we want our coachees to feel.

Questions which the coach asks as part of the contracting process prepare the way for what will be explored and how this exploration will happen.

Contracting creates clarity and direction, and increases coachee engagement

2. Start with an Update

From the second session onwards, there's an opportunity to start asking the coachee for an update on their progress or actions taken since the last time you met. This conversation is important, as it often informs the focus for the upcoming session. For example:

Coach: "How did you get on with the actions you set at the end of our last session?"

Coachee: "Not too bad with most tasks, but I struggled with having a conversation with my line manager about taking on more responsibilities."

Coach: "Tell me more about that."

Coachee: "Well, despite saying in our last session that I thought I'd be able to tell her what I want, when it came to it, I just couldn't bring myself to do it."

Coach: "What do you think stopped you?"

Coachee: "She might not think I'm good enough to take on more projects."

Coach: "I'm curious, what's your evidence that she might not think you're good enough to take on more projects?"

Coachee: "Err… I don't know… I'm not sure I have any. I just have a feeling."

Coach: "So, thinking about the session ahead of us, and your preparation before you came here today, what would be a good use of our time?"

Coachee: "Well… as my goal is to further my career to a senior leadership role, it will probably be useful to explore how I can approach my line manager to have the conversation I obviously need to have!"

Coach: "OK, so what would you like to have achieved by the end of our session?"

Coachee: "I think I'd like to have discussed some different options, and come up with at least one that I feel confident to carry out."

Coach:	"Great. I noticed you said, 'at least one that I feel confident to carry out.' How important is feeling confident in this situation to you?"
Coachee:	"Really important... thinking about why I didn't do my task... perhaps it's me who doesn't think I'm good enough, rather than my line manager."

This was taken from my third coaching session with a coachee who was working in an organisation. If I hadn't asked for an update at the start of this session, we may not have arrived at this insight until later in the coaching process, if at all.

Before we went any further here, I also checked on the other tasks that had been successfully carried out. Successes shouldn't be ignored as they can shed light on useful information, such as highlighting a particular strength or an approach to tasks that may be useful in the future.

Other update questions include:

- What actions have you achieved since we last met?

- What was the impact of these actions?
- What wider impact, if any, did you notice?
- Where else have you made progress?
- What general reflections have you had since our last session?

Update questions are a useful way to build a coachee's engagement in a session, as it is starting with *them* – their experiences, thoughts and insights. As a result of following this through, they "own" the focus for the session; it's not given to them.

What happens when none of the coachee's actions have been carried out?

Sometimes there are very good reasons why a coachee hasn't carried out their action(s). For example:

- They've been ill.
- Someone else who was involved in the completion of the action was unwell or unavailable.
- The task was linked to a project that has been stopped.
- Something else in the coachee's life has occurred that had to take priority (e.g. an unexpected family situation).

I know coaches who will offer to postpone a coaching session when something beyond the coachee's control has occurred to prevent them from completing a task, which could still be done with a little more time.

This is up to you. Just be mindful that you need to ensure momentum continues in some format, such as agreed email updates, otherwise this lack of progress risks coachee engagement.

If you still meet with your coachee when they haven't progressed with their task(s), it still provides an opportunity to work on another part of their goal, or an alternative way to achieve the same result they were aiming for in the previous session.

What happens when a coachee repeatedly arrives at a coaching session not having completed their actions?

This needs to be addressed, as it *could* call into question their level of commitment to coaching and engagement in the process itself. I like to try and nip this in the bud when it occurs twice in a row. The reason for lack of action is something along the lines of, "I've just not had the time."

When setting actions at the end of a coaching session, time to complete them needs to be factored in. Sufficient time should be devoted to ensuring any actions that continue the coachee's development towards their goal are explored and appropriately planned to increase the likelihood of completion.

So how could you address the coachee's lack of action? Here are some examples:

Questions to Address Inaction

- What has stopped you from completing your action from our last session?

- What thoughts did you have about your action(s), after we set them at the end of our last session?

- When we set the action(s) at the end of today's session, how should we do this so that there's a greater chance of you being able to achieve it?

- What do you notice about how you set goals in general, not just in coaching? What do you find is the most effective way to achieve them?

The questions here aren't meant to negatively challenge or judge the coachee, or make any accusations about their lack of engagement in the process. Remember, as coaches, we're still working from a place of unconditional positive regard for our coachees, and we want them to succeed!

The questions above are meant to shine a light on how the coachee could work best to set and achieve actionable steps that will help them move forward. Exploring their motivators would also be a useful conversation to have, building these into the planning and execution of the action.

If, having had this conversation, the coachee continues to lack engagement and fails to complete further actions they have set for themselves, then a conversation needs to take place around how useful coaching is for them right now.

Ask them directly how useful they are finding the sessions, and what they are taking away from the process. Their answers should show you both whether it's worth continuing or not.

3. Start with a Check-in

Coaching check-ins are optional short exercises at the start of a session, and I personally love them! They are really powerful ways to begin a coaching session for three reasons:

1. They help a coachee become present for their coaching session, bridging the gap between their previous activity and being coached. Check-ins work particularly well in grounding a coachee when they arrive with their mind still processing, or distracted by, their previous activity.

2. They have the ability to help identify how a coachee is feeling or showing up at the start of the session. In my experience, this has ranged from calm or excited and prepared for the session to totally unprepared with their mind elsewhere.

3. They help identify a topic for coaching if a coachee arrives not knowing what they want to talk about. This often happens when the coachee has booked a block of coaching sessions without a specific overall goal (or it's simply ongoing personal development). They know the benefits that coaching can bring, and enjoy that personal time focused totally on themselves.

Coaching Check-in Example

1. Using Image Cards or Image Sets

There are a wide variety of packs of postcards or playing card-sized cards that you can buy that have images on them intended to promote creative, abstract or associative thinking.

Packs can have themes (such as Mindfulness, Values or Strengths), or can be more miscellaneous. I prefer the latter when working with coachees, as they provide a wider scope for thinking. But the themed ones can be more helpful when the coachee has a goal that's focused on that theme, such as 'strengths' when their goal is career-based.

The best image cards have an image on one side and a question on the other, usually with some sort of connection, giving you the option to use one or both sides of the card. Here's an example:

The image might be an owl sitting in a tree. The question on the back might say, "Which choices have you made in your life that have been wise?"

Of course you may have chosen the owl because you liked the colour of its feathers, or it's brought to mind the idea of "freedom." It doesn't really matter.

Using these cards is quite simple. Start by spreading some or all of the cards out on a table, or invite the coachee to look through the pack, and choose a card that represents one of the following:

- How they are feeling right now
- How they are showing up for the session
- Progress they've made since the last session
- What they're looking forward to most in today's session

Some coachees like to choose more than one! I usually limit it to three so the activity doesn't take up too much time. Providing a limit also helps to focus their thoughts on what's most important to them right now.

Ask the coachee to share their reason(s) for their choice(s), giving them time to share without interruption or judgement.

Remember, one of the great things about this activity is that there's no wrong answer!

You could also have three people in a group-coaching session who want the same card for completely different reasons. Here's an example:

A picture of a set of lit candles could be chosen in answer to the question, "How are you showing up for this coaching session?" for the following reasons:

1. I'm showing up calm and ready to shine a light on my successes since our last session.

2. I'm feeling like I need ideas in today's session, and the flames represent ideas I will have.

3. I see the three different sized candles representing the different stages of my growth towards my goal.

Often the responses will tap into some relevant theme linked to the coachee's goal that would benefit from further exploration in the session.

Take the third example above. I would follow this up with a question that invites the coachee to say more about the three stages. There could be something in their response that identifies a focus for the session. For example, they're at the final stage and are finding it a struggle. You can then go into the "struggle" in more depth, and if appropriate, use this as the focus for the session

Other benefits of this check-in activity include:

- It's great for people who learn, and like to represent their thoughts, visually.
- It's received well by coachees who sometimes find maintaining eye contact difficult. This type of activity gives them something else to focus on whilst also maintaining their engagement.
- As a resource, there are lots of different ones to choose from.
- You can make your own!

I've created several image sets covering different themes, printed them out and laminated them. Each set is usually 16 to 20 images arranged on a single, one-sided A4 document.

Use the link or scan the QR code below to see image set examples, with some available to download for your own use.

https://go.theleadershipcoachingacademy.com/bookresources

I am also able to use these as "image slides" when coaching online. I share my screen and ask the coachee to choose an image as if we were in the same room.

What other potential can you see for using image sets?

2. Using Question Cards

As well as image cards with questions on the back, you can also source card packs which have a thought-provoking question on each card.

You'll often find that the questions have a coaching-style about them, and can add to your own tool kit of questions, such as:

- What's the most useful thing you've done towards your goal this week?

- Who have you supported recently? What impact did this have?

- What have you learned about yourself this week?

I've used these in two different ways:

1. Spread them out and ask the coachee to choose one.

2. Give the coachee the set of cards turned over so that they can only see the backs of the cards. Ask them to choose three cards randomly. Once chosen, they look at the questions and choose *one* to answer.

3. "Permission to…" Cards

I've not actually come across these to buy, but I've seen them being used, which prompted me to create my own.

"Permission to…" cards contain phrases that invite you to give yourself permission to be, do, say or feel something, and are very useful at the start of a coaching session. They help to gauge how a coachee is feeling, and can help inform how you coach them in that session. For example:

- Permission to let go

- Permission to have fun

- Permission to be myself

- Permission to start again

- Permission to be creative

- Permission to fail and learn

- Permission to be vulnerable

- Permission to be challenged

- Permission to stop and think

- Permission to have lots of ideas

If they start the session giving themselves permission to be challenged, for example, I would follow this up by asking:

- "What will 'being challenged' look, feel or sound like for you in today's session?"

- "What is 'challenge' about for you today?"

- "How can I best support you to (feel) challenged in this session?"

These (and similar) follow-up questions help the coachee go deeper into the detail of their thinking, create clearer pictures of what they mean and increase their level of engagement in their own learning.

Self-Reflective Questions:

Which of the three types of cards described above do you prefer?

Which might your coachees prefer?

Summary

- The coaching session needs to provide a structure that supports the coachee's goal achievement.

- Clear, confident starts include some form of contracting that generates the session's focus, desired outcome and perceived value in the coaching process for the coachee.

- Clear starts can also include updates that discuss progress, and optional check-in exercises that add variety to the creative thinking process.

- Going into greater depth on the session outcome encourages the coachee to connect more with their goal, which increases their engagement in the process.

- A focused start also maximises the time available, thereby increasing perceived value for money or value for the time spent.

Actions

1. Review how you carry out your contracting process in the first and subsequent coaching sessions.

How clear is the start of your session? How clear are both you and the coachee on the outcomes of the session that you're working towards?

2. Reflect on your approach to addressing inaction with coachees.

   How could you address this moving forward?

3. Introduce variety!

   If your coaching sessions generally start the same way, and you've worked with a coachee for a number of sessions, offer them alternative ways to "check into" the session to see what they prefer. It helps give them even more control of their learning and engagement in the process.

Part 3: Maintaining Engagement

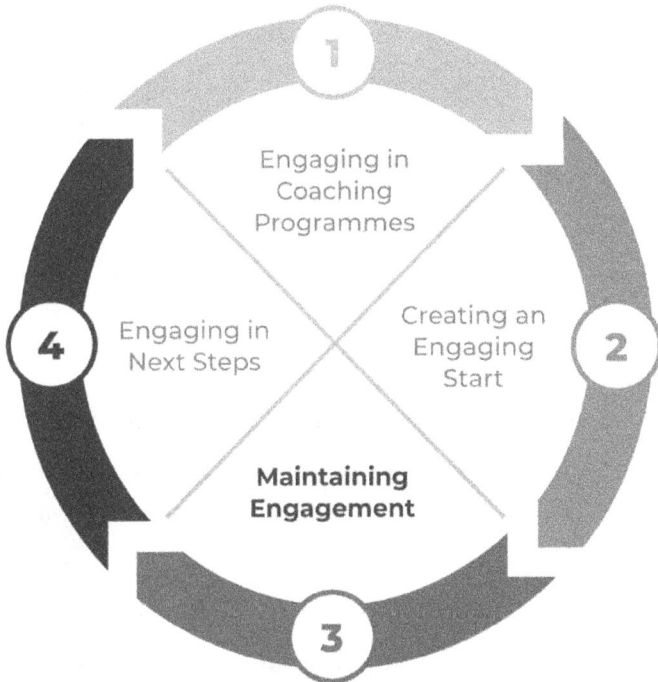

Engaging in
Coaching
Programmes

Creating an
Engaging
Start

Engaging in
Next Steps

**Maintaining
Engagement**

Once your coaching session has got off to a positive and productive start, preserving this high level of engagement to maximise outcomes will involve different things from coach and coachee.

It's worth reminding ourselves here that we're only human, and we're working with coachees who are also human! Thoughts and behaviours will, at times, inevitably intrude into us operating at our best.

Things will happen in coaching sessions that we feel could have gone better, or that we might have done differently.

So how might this present itself?

Scenario 1

> You're in the middle of a coaching session and you notice that the flow you had at the start has reduced or disappeared altogether. Things feel different. You've noticed a dip in the coachee's level of engagement. Your senses are picking up a shift in their body language; they look less comfortable. They're also giving you shorter answers.

Scenario 2

> Alternatively, you find yourself distracted.
> You're not concentrating as much as you were
> before, and you find that this is impacting on
> your ability to actively listen, as you try and
> unpick what's going on. Are you being
> distracted by something externally (something
> about the coachee or something in the
> environment)? Or is it something internal, such
> as distracting thoughts?

Whatever the signs, the key identifier for you is that
something is different; something has changed with the
coachee, you or both.

In this third part of the book, I will explore some of the
reasons for reduced flow and a lack of engagement,
surprisingly not all of which are detrimental to coaching
success.

Some will arise as a result of the coachee's thoughts and
behaviours; others will be due to the coach's mindset
and practice

Let's start with you, the coach!

Maintaining high engagement involves different things from coach and coachee

Chapter 4
How Coaches Can Disrupt Engagement

In this chapter, I will explore three ways in which our own engagement in a coaching session can dip, and how we can also disrupt the coachee's level of engagement and focus.

I'll also offer practical ideas and ways of thinking in response to these potential disruptions.

Perhaps the most common disruptor for the coach, which I've found from my supervision sessions and conversations with other coaches, is self-doubt. So I'll start with that.

1. Self-doubt

You've done your coaching training, you have the skills and you can coach. You want to do a good job and give value to your coachees, but you have doubts.

What might these be, and how do they impact on your ability to engage fully in the coaching process?

From my own practice, and from supervising other coaches, doubts generally come from a lack of experience or a lack of self-belief. You need more evidence that you've done a good job, and you're just not there yet.

Our ego also wants to be seen to be doing a good job too. "Look at me. Aren't I great?!" Or, "My coachees need to see that my services are worth paying for.

The issue with self-doubt and an ego focus is that we can carry these thoughts into our sessions and, without meaning to, put too much attention on ourselves to "get it right." We're too inwardly focused. Although we're the facilitators in this process, it's not about us.

I've been here a few times, and occasionally still recognise when I'm heading towards "doubting Debbie." I may have had a bad day. I may not be feeling one hundred percent, or as resourceful and creative as I usually do.

Whatever the reason for our doubts, it can impact our confidence and certainty, which can "leak" out in a coaching session and be noticed by our coachees.

Although we're
the facilitators
in the coaching
process, it's not
about us!

Like us, coachees can sense subtle changes in body language and tone, even subconsciously. They'll notice our trepidation and may hold back from sharing things that are particularly sensitive, or things that make them appear vulnerable. This, in turn, can result in a lack of depth to the coaching session, not uncovering what's key to continued progress and not maximising the time available. And of course, this also impacts on their level of engagement.

So how do we manage self-doubt? Below are some helpful tips.

Gather Evidence About Your Practice

Do this routinely by asking coachees for feedback or testimonials. You can also build in questions such as, "What have you gained from this coaching session or programme of sessions?"

Capturing their feedback here could be the foundations of a testimonial, which you can send them and ask if their comments are OK to use – either with their name or anonymously if they prefer. It's better than asking them for a testimonial, which involves them starting with a blank piece of paper. I've often found that coachees are more than happy to use the comments I've captured as a starting point.

And, by the way, what's "enough" evidence? How much evidence do you need in order to believe in yourself, and be fully and confidently engaged in the coaching process?

Another way to gather evidence is during your own session review. Have somewhere you make a note of the things you did well. Include notes on when you were operating at your best; what were you thinking, feeling and doing?

Read these notes and one or two testimonials whenever you feel self-doubt creeping in, or you find yourself needing a confidence boost.

Give Yourself a Good Talking To

Our self-doubt generally presents itself as internal dialogue, or the things we say to ourselves. This dialogue can include:

- How "good" or "bad" we believe our skills are.
- What we believe we're capable of for a particular situation.
- Why something will or won't work, based on our 'evidence' of a previous event.

I have two responses to this:

1. What would you say to a coachee who was displaying self-doubt? What questions would you ask them? What could you ask yourself?

2. Write down your internal dialogue, then create an alternative dialogue you'd prefer to be saying that would result in you giving a great, confident service to your coachees.

Self-Reflective Questions:

What have you *already* tried?

What would be most useful for you to do?

Design and Wear Your "Coaching Coat"

We all have different roles in our lives, whether it be parent, daughter, nephew, friend, pet owner, leader, team member, entrepreneur, mentor, or coach – and each role involves its own thinking and behaviours. These come from different ways we perceive that role, plus what's expected of us by the other stakeholders involved.

Adopting each role is often subconscious and feels seamless, especially those roles we've done for years.

In the early part of your coaching career, you may need to spend longer preparing to be "a coach" leading up to your sessions, as you remind yourself what the different elements of your role are.

To help in this process, the larger coaching organisations provide codes of conduct and core competencies, which help create our coaching "identity."

For me, despite how useful this guidance is, in written format it can feel a little dry. So over the years I've found it helpful to create something that reminds me of the key features of my role that provide me with clarity, confidence and resourcefulness, whilst also dampening or removing any self-doubt.

It helps me be the best version of myself as a "coach" for my coachees.

It's my "coaching coat" and it comes out of its wardrobe when I'm preparing for a coaching session that I'm feeling less confident about.

Let me paint a picture of it for you…

Back of Coat

This represents my most confident state. It has my back, so to speak. When I put my coaching coat on, I feel its support. There's a calmness, a positive energy and a readiness to coach exuding from it.

I've worked on this over time and tweaked it as I've learned what is my most confident coaching state.

Oh, and it's also purple! This is my favourite colour, but represents creativity, wisdom and peace – particularly being at peace with myself.

Sleeves and Cuffs

These represent communication and control. Communication is about my coaching questions, summaries and general responses (including non-verbal).

In my everyday life, I use gestures and talk with my hands. So when I meet a coachee who does not do this when they're communicating, I need to "fasten my cuffs" as a reminder to control my arms and hands.

This also goes for my verbal language. When building rapport with coachees, especially in the first few sessions, it's important to pay attention to the words and phrases a coachee uses. I listen carefully to mirror and match their language in my questions and summaries, rather than substituting their words with my own interpretations, which might have a different meaning for the coachee.

Front Sections and Pockets

These represent my front-facing professionalism as a coach (side sections), and my coaching toolkit (pockets).

The professionalism element is made up of coaching principles, including things like confidentiality, ethics and my belief in the coachee and their capabilities.

The pockets have grown deeper over the years as I've added more tools to my coaching toolkit. When I put my coaching coat on, I remind myself of the coachee's focus area and which tools I can introduce to the coachee which may be of benefit to them.

In terms of using tools, I'm a firm believer in sharing a tool and how it works, saying why I think it could help in this session and then offering the tool as an option. It's the coachee's decision whether or not they will want to use it; I don't presume.

Collar

This is for holding my affirmations, as it's the closest part of the coat to my ear, so I'll "hear" them.

Affirmations that have helped me in the past include:

- I am a trained and experienced coach who has the skills to help and support my coachees.

- I am feeling resourceful today, and trust that the right questions and tools will come to me when required.

- I am calm, confident and ready to coach.

Hidden Inside Pocket

I love a secret pocket, don't you?

Here I store my "getting unstuck" questions. These are questions I use when I feel stuck in a coaching session.

Questions and reasons why I use them include:

- "Sorry, I got momentarily distracted by that (loud bang), would you mind saying that again?"

- This is just about being honest when you get distracted by something, rather than bluff your way out of it with a random question, hoping the coachee won't notice (that rarely works!).

- "What's most important to you right now / about all of this?"
  - I use this kind of question when the coachee has talked for a while, raising several topics, and I'm not sure which of these to ask them about. So this question helps identify where to go next in the session.

- "If I were to ask you a really brilliant question right now, what would it be?"
  - This is a really good question to ask in a session anyway, but I might ask this if I genuinely can't think of a question, or am doubting that any other question I can think of is "good enough."

Which questions are in your hidden inside pocket?

Coat Alternatives

The above is obviously a description of my coaching coat. What would yours be like?

- It could be a jacket, shirt, cardigan or any favourite item of clothing you wear when you coach – so you're *actually* wearing it rather than metaphorically wearing it!
- Your coat could be made up of different parts of one key element, such as your "most confident coaching state."
- It could adopt different colours depending on how you're feeling before each session, like blue or green when you want to have a calm approach, or yellow or orange if you need an energy boost.
- It could have a patchwork quilt effect, where each square represents something different.

Adapt your coat as you become more experienced so that it continues to "fit you well." Take the metaphor as far as you like!

My coaching coat now generally protects me from self-doubt, and reinforces my coaching persona.

What does your coaching coat look like?

2. The Mentoring Trap

Those who move into coaching from another profession have often come from management or team leader positions, and so have used mentoring before. So, it takes a while to adjust to the idea that they don't need to know another person's role in order to coach them successfully. As we know, it's not about telling the coachee what to do, or offering solutions to the coachee's problems.

From training and working with new coaches, the issue is often around the mindset of "helping." People generally go into coaching because they want to help others, and traditionally helping is about giving in some way, such as

- Giving advice: "You'd really benefit from downloading this relaxation app."
- Sharing the benefit of your experience: "When I was in your shoes, I did (x) and it worked really well!"
- Giving ideas or options that will help the other person solve their problem: "Have you thought about blocking out time in your diary, or creating a To Do list, or saying 'no' to other things, so you can get this project finished on time?"

Putting it simply, mentoring involves the mentor having experience in the area that the mentee wants to develop, and sharing this experience. Coaching involves the coach using a particular mindset and set of skills to help the coachee find their own solutions and ways forward.

Both are equally valid and have their place in people development. But it's important that coach and coachee know the difference, so there's no confusion about each person's role in the coaching session.

"Menching"

When we start to learn about how coaching is different to mentoring, we learn that asking questions is the best replacement for telling a person what they could do.

Example scenario:

> A coachee's goal is to improve their confidence in speaking to groups of colleagues as part of their new management role. They've told their coach that they struggle with speaking clearly and confidently, as nerves get the better of them.
>
> A coach with some experience might ask here: "What's at the core of this for you?", to get to the specifics of the issue.

A new coach, immediately thinking of offering a tip they've found useful, but also recognising that coaching is about asking not telling, responds with, "How might planning and visualising a confident version of you speaking at your next group meeting help?"

Yes, it's a question, but it's also a suggestion. The coach in the latter scenario is caught between offering a helpful idea and knowing they should be asking a question.

They're moving from **men**toring into coa**ching** – or as I like to call it: **Menching**!

Like all new things, it's a developmental process, and evolves by maintaining a coaching mindset, trusting the coaching process and practice.

A coaching mindset includes:

- Understanding that the coachee is responsible for their goals and choice of actions.
- Focusing on what the coachee thinks and experiences, without the coach imposing their own thoughts or feelings.
- Believing the coachee has the answers within them and they are capable of achieving more.

- Trusting that the coachee's self-knowledge and increased self-awareness improves their performance.

So, when does menching impact engagement in the coaching session?

Once you're established as a coach and are using a coaching approach as standard practice, your coachees will become used to being in control of, and valuing, their own solutions that you've helped them create.

But what if, during a coaching session, you find yourself suddenly offering a suggestion?

This could be down to lack of concentration or you just can't think of a question at that moment and you panic, feeling the need to fill a silence. So, in order to maintain a helpful presence, you offer an idea.

In my experience, I can *see* what happens to a coachee when I've shifted from coaching to menching. They've been used to feeling the power of pure coaching and all its benefits, and now (worst case scenario) it appears I don't trust them enough to come up with their own ideas. This shift in their thinking is apparent from a change in their body language, facial expressions or hesitation before speaking.

It's also worth saying, I'm very easy to coach! I clearly know my role, as well as the coach's. And when a coach has offered me a suggestion in the past, the best way I can describe it is I've felt a dip in my enthusiasm and energy. I've wanted to experience the joy and empowerment of coming to my own solution. I try to politely decline their suggestion and get the conversation back on track to focusing on *my* ideas.

So, how can we avoid menching?

With more experience comes fewer instances where this creeps in. You have more questions in your toolkit and strategies to avoid the mentoring trap.

Good preparation for coaching includes having a bank of questions you could ask when you feel the urge to offer an idea.

Some questions I've found helpful include:

- If I were to offer you a suggestion right now that would be really helpful, what would it be?
- What would a trusted colleague advise you to do?
- If you had no fear, what would be your next step?

These are all great questions from the "options" section of the GROW model that I've included in the "References" in the back of this book. Sometimes it's just worth spending a bit more time in this part of the coaching process to generate a range of options from which the coachee can choose.

Ultimately it's about trusting the coaching process. Your training should have provided you with the mindset and skills to deliver an effective coaching session with a willing coachee.

Trust
the
process!

3. Lack of Challenge for Growth

I love this quote from Canfield and Chee (2013):

"If you feel a lack of challenge in a coaching relationship, both you and the client may just be sailing along on a light breeze, enjoying the conversation but not achieving much."

Coaching is about moving forward in some way towards the coachee's desired outcome, usually referred to as their "goal." Without forward movement, the coachee risks not seeing the value of coaching, thereby becoming disengaged.

Once we've identified our coachee's goal or outcome for the coaching programme, a key part of our role is to help them overcome obstacles that have so far slowed or halted their progress.

This involves challenge combined with support, which can be illustrated by the Challenge-Support Grid.

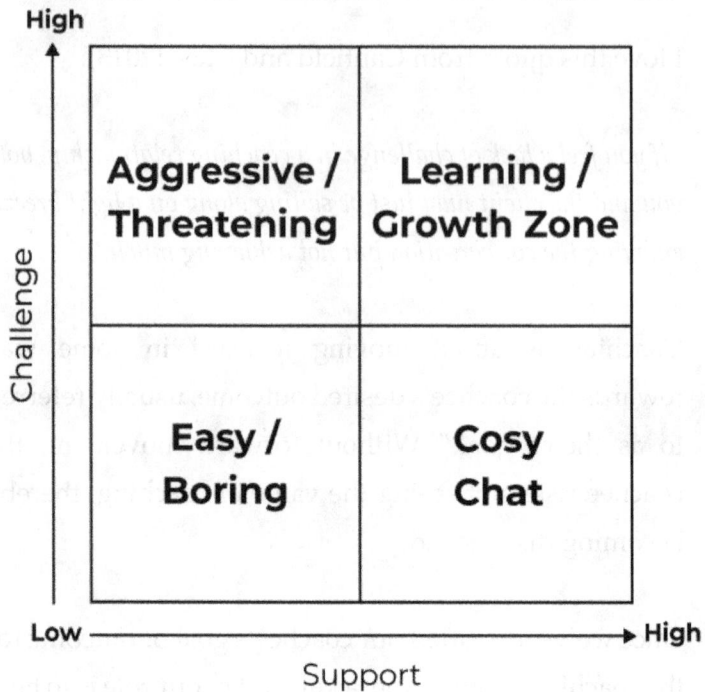

The features of each area include:

Easy / Boring: Low Challenge, Low Support

- May look distracted or bored
- Short answers without little thought behind them
- Little or no investment or engagement in the process
- Whole process may feel mundane

Aggressive / Threatening: High Challenge, Low Support

- Little or no rapport
- No opportunities to explore coachee's strengths
- Coachee doesn't feel valued or understood; may feel stressed
- Questioning of the coachee's goals and limiting beliefs, but without acknowledging any progress

Cosy Chat: Low Challenge, High Support

- Friendly, conversational chat
- Lots of empathy and understanding
- Little or no challenge of the coachee's thoughts or beliefs that may be holding them back
- Nothing much has changed by the end of the conversation

Learning / Growth Zone: High Challenge, High Support

- Progress by the end of the session is evident
- Good level of rapport, deeper levels of listening, and intuitive questioning
- Strong engagement with the coachee being highly invested in the session outcomes
- The coachee understands there's a positive intent behind the coach's probing questions,

which are for their benefit, growth and development

Which zone do you spend the most time in during your coaching sessions?

Using the right balance of challenge and support will facilitate the coachee's progress, and even small steps towards their goal can maintain and even increase engagement.

Sometimes, particularly as new coaches, we can be afraid to challenge coachees, for fear of overstepping the mark and appearing aggressive, when it's clearly not our intention. Knowing the key features of the challenge-support grid can show us what we're working towards (which is the "Learning/Growth Zone"), and also recognise when we've gone too far the other way ("Cosy", "Boring" or "Aggressive" zones).

Productive challenge in our coaching sessions will generate progress and success, which will increase the coachee's engagement and desire for more.

Productive challenge in our coaching sessions will generate progress and success

Let's look at times when we can offer challenge and what that might look like.

Challenging the Goal

It's crucial that the coachee's goal will stretch them personally or professionally, although one will usually influence the other.

In my early years as a coach, I was working with a senior leader who happily identified their goal, and as we talked through what they'd done towards it so far, they'd clearly already achieved it. The reasons for their choice of goal is perhaps for another book, but it was a valuable lesson learned. I definitely missed asking some key questions to ensure the goal was future-focused and something the coachee was working towards.

I've since learned to ask questions such as these below to help identify suitable goals:

- How will this goal stretch you?
- How will achieving this goal support your professional or personal development?
- What will be different?
- How will achieving this goal impact your role?
- What other impact might you notice?

Challenging Limiting Beliefs

What we believe about ourselves and our capabilities will limit us to act within the boundaries of these beliefs and achieve little else. Our coachees often come to coaching having hit an obstacle, and they're struggling to make progress on their own.

Here are a few statements I've heard coachees make, along with potential responses that could be offered in return.

Coachee statements:

- "I'll *never* make a good manager!"
- "I'm hopeless at leading meetings."
- "It's too difficult."
- "I'm bound to make a mess of it. What's the point?"
- "I'm just not a confident speaker."

Coach responses:

- "How do you know?"
- "What's your evidence that you're hopeless?"
- "What makes it difficult?"
- "And if there was a point, what would it be?"
- "What examples can you think of that would contradict that?"

On paper, the question examples above may come across as harsh or aggressive, but not if your tone of voice is professional and supportive.

Try saying the responses in different ways.

Which comes across as most authentic and supportive?

And of course, some of the responses above are interchangeable, with the odd word change.

As coaches, we *must* get comfortable with offering challenge here. Our coachees are counting on us to do so – although they may not realise it yet! We need to delve into the meaning behind their statements, and uncover the belief that's holding them back, so we can facilitate their progress and subsequent success.

Self-Reflective Questions:

On a scale of 1 to 10, how comfortable are you with challenging your coachees?

Which of the challenge responses above could you add to your toolkit?

Summary

- As coaches, we can manage self-doubt by gathering evidence of our successes, change unhelpful inner dialogue, or create a "coaching coat" that represents our best coaching state, and which we wear to counter any emerging confidence dips.

- When we offer a coachee suggestions, we're denying them the opportunity to find their own solutions, increase their resourcefulness and boost their self-belief in overcoming hurdles.

- With experience comes fewer tendencies to dip into mentoring and offer a coachee suggestions or ideas. In the meantime, it's useful to have a few "anti-mentoring" questions that put the focus back on the coachee to come up with their own solutions.

- The right balance of challenge and support generates new insights and growth for coachees. When aligned with their goals, it creates momentum, which sustains and often increases engagement.

Actions

1. Choose a strategy for managing self-doubt.

    Use the ideas in this chapter or create one of your own. Have it ready, just in case you approach a coaching session lacking self-belief for whatever reason. Most importantly–be kind to yourself and remind yourself that we're all human!

2. Review your definition of "helping" in a coaching context.

    This is especially the case if you've been used to mentoring and have a tendency to use a blended "coaching and mentoring" approach. Create a definition that helps you trust the coachee to find their own solutions.

3. Become familiar with the kind of questions that help a coachee find their own solutions.

    This will help avoid falling into the mentoring trap, or menching!

4. Choose some questions that will challenge the coachee's goal and any limiting beliefs that may arise.

Use the questions suggested in this chapter as a starting point, until you find ones that come most naturally to you in the moment.

5. Talk about challenge with your coachee.

    You can do this in the pre-coaching conversation with a coachee who has experience of coaching, and understands what "challenge" in coaching means. Ask them how they prefer to be challenged, but also be flexible, as you may discover other successful ways to challenge them.

    With a coachee who's not experienced coaching before, wait until you've done one or two coaching sessions, before discussing how challenge plays an important role in coaching, and where you may have already been doing this in your sessions. Ask them how they've found the level of challenge relevant to their goal, and adapt your practice accordingly.

Chapter 5
What to Do When a
Coachee is Stuck

During my initial research for this book, I asked coaches what kind of challenges they face during coaching sessions, and the most common answer was: "What to do when a coachee gets stuck."

By being "stuck" they referred to a coachee's response being:

- "I don't know."

- "I'm not sure."

- "I can't think of anything."

This can feel uncomfortable, halting the flow and risking coachee engagement, particularly when *you're* not sure how to respond. In other words: YOU are now stuck too!

Imagine the scenario...

> The coachee has been talking about a tricky situation with a colleague which led to a confrontation. They work with this person on a daily basis and are worried that it could happen again.

> Coach: "What could you do to avoid this situation in the future?"

> Coachee: [After a long pause] "I just don't know..."

> [Then looks directly back at you, waiting for you to speak]

> Coach: [Thinking] OK, so how do I respond to this?

> I can't give them ideas, that's not coaching. Even if I did suggest something "just this once," they might come to expect suggestions from me whenever they don't readily have an answer. This isn't going to help them grow and build their own resourcefulness.

All I can think of right now is "Why don't you know?" However, if I ask "why," I risk sounding judgemental and overly challenging. But I can't just sit here and say nothing!

Sound familiar?

As a result of this inner dialogue, you might resort to accepting their response, and moving on to something else, rather than offering a suggestion or pursuing their response further because it feels too challenging and you don't want to lose rapport.

In this scenario, it can feel natural to ask more questions about the coachee's current situation or go back to the goal and explore that in more depth, because you're doing something constructive.

But what if you come back around to the same topic (e.g. avoiding a confrontation, as in the example above), and the coachee has the same answer as before? How would you respond next time?

I used to dread the times in a coaching session when a coachee responded to a question with, "I don't know." I preferred and enjoyed the flow of question - answer - question - answer.

Now I recognise and embrace these stuck moments as opportunities for growth. They lead to:

- New insights
- Creative thinking
- Increased confidence
- Further development of the coachee's resourcefulness

Perhaps like you, I enjoy hearing, "That's a great question!" from a coachee, rather than "I don't know." Nevertheless, they're two sides of the same coin. They both indicate that the coachee is at some sort of threshold in their learning.

"That's a great question!" possesses a level of energy or excitement, and the coachee is embracing the chance to think it through and provide a considered answer. Whereas "I don't know" suggests they need prompting or further support to provide an answer.

There is the flip side of this type of response where the coachee simply doesn't *want* to answer that particular question. In this chapter, I'd like to delve further into what's behind the "I don't know" responses, starting with what we mean by "stuck" in a coaching session.

Defining "Stuck"

The dictionary defines stuck as, "to be at a standstill, as from difficulties."

When we meet coachees, they are usually at some sort of standstill or feel like they're going around in circles. In either case, there's no forward movement, despite their best intentions, having tried different strategies which are either their own or have been suggested by others.

Once we start coaching, the purpose of the main goal is to move the coachee beyond their point of "standstill" to their desired outcome. Within this journey you will undoubtedly encounter the obstacle or obstacles that have halted the coachee's progress previously.

This leads us to the first type of "stuck" that exists within a coaching session:

1. The coachee simply can't think of an answer to your question.

I also believe there's another scenario where the coachee can appear to be stuck:

2. They have an answer but are choosing not to share it.

Let's look at each of these in turn, with some suggestions for how to respond.

1. The Coachee Can't Think of an Answer to Your Question

This feels like genuine "stuckness"; they appear to be thinking about the question and how to respond, looking around searching for an answer, accessing different parts of their brains to do so. Eventually they look back at you, and tell you they don't know.

Below I've detailed some possible solutions to this dilemma.

The Question Approach

This fits in nicely with all the other questions you ask coachees in response to the thoughts and feelings they provide during your conversations.

In your coach training course, you may have come across helpful examples of responses to "I don't know" or "I can't think of anything," such as:

- "And what if you *did* know?"

- "And what if you *could* think of something?"

- "What might a trusted colleague or someone who knows you well suggest?"

You probably recognise the questions above from the Options section of the GROW Model (found in the References section of this book), as well as other similar models which allow the coachee to create and consider different ways forward.

Here are some more that I've used:

- "So how could we approach this from a different perspective?"

- "How could we look at this more creatively?"

- "Let's say that by the end of this coaching session we have a solution, how might we have got there?"

- "When I asked you, 'What could you do in that situation?', what would have been a better question?"

These questions help to generate "possibility thinking" for the coachee, which widens the coachee's perception of what can be achieved.

Recognise and
embrace these
stuck moments
as opportunities
for growth

Changing the Environment

If questions aren't working, perhaps a change of setting will help. Whenever I'm stuck with my own thoughts, I go to a different room in the house or go for a walk. I'll either resume my thoughts in the new environment, if it feels easy enough to do so, or do something different, thereby taking a break and giving my head time to generate capacity for more productive thinking later.

So what opportunities do you have to change the coaching environment?

If walking outside is an option, and the coachee is in agreement, then it's worth re-contracting for how you will spend this time, including how long you'll be outside for. By re-contracting, the walk will have a purpose even if that's simply getting some fresh air for five minutes.

Once outside, coachees benefit from:

- No physical barriers, which expands thinking opportunities.
- The act of walking, which boosts blood flow to the brain and increases creative output.

- Not having direct eye contact with their coach, so they feel less "in the spotlight" and are likely to be more open and honest.

If the re-contracting process has elicited the opportunity to continue coaching them outside on their goal, questions you could ask include:

- What do you notice in this environment that represents your goal?

- What represents being stuck?

- As we're walking, what do you notice that is significant? What makes it so?

- What else are you noticing or sensing that is worth mentioning?

These and other questions you ask may create metaphors for the coachee, which you can explore further to help them become unstuck, or uncover something else useful.

If going outside isn't an option, where else in the building can you move to? And if working online or on the phone, could they move around the room they're in?

The Proactive Approach

As well as responding in the moment, as in the first two solutions above, you can also raise the concept of being stuck openly with your coachee before it arises, namely:

- During the informal contracting part, when you discuss how you'll work together, or

- At the start of the first session, as part of contracting for that session.

I almost hesitate to suggest having this conversation before the coachee actually becomes stuck. It risks putting the idea in the coachee's head that they will inevitably get stuck, when they may not.

However, I balance this with the knowledge that being stuck is both a necessary and a useful part of the growth process, which coaching facilitates.

What you might say during the initial contracting conversation:

- "Part of the coaching process includes addressing any obstacles that may arise as we work towards your goal. When you've come across obstacles in the past, how do you usually address them?"

- "If you feel stuck in one of our sessions, what would be a good way to work through this until you're no longer stuck?"

- "Given that coaching isn't about me giving you answers or telling you what to do, how would you like me to respond or support you if you get stuck?"

Self-Reflective Question:

What else might you say that fits in with how you currently contract in coaching?

Use contracting
opportunities
to discuss
how to address
being stuck

2. The Coachee Has an Answer but Is Choosing Not to Share It

What might be behind this? Here are some hypotheses:

- The coachee isn't used to being asked such probing questions and feels uncomfortable sharing their thoughts. The questions they've already asked themselves, or been asked by others, have been more "surface level," and involved little depth of thinking. This is usually their first coaching experience.

- The coachee may be struggling to find an answer because they lack confidence, either in themselves or more specifically their ability to achieve their goal. Answering certain questions may result in feelings of vulnerability, and they are not ready to go there – at least not yet.

- The coachee doesn't trust you enough yet to open up and share information that feels personal, or are concerned about what happens to that information, particularly when they've been offered coaching by their line manager.

Please note – not all coachees in organisations are *offered* coaching; some are *sent* to a coach who's either working internally or has been brought in from outside the organisation. In this scenario, it can take longer to develop a positive, supportive and developmental relationship where the coachee trusts the process – and their coach! Transparency is key, as I shared in Chapter 1 as part of the Pre-Coaching Conversation.

Perhaps you're already thinking, "The solution is rapport!" And I'd agree. Having a good level of rapport will help you build trust (along with maintaining confidentiality), and create the environment in which the coachee feels able to explore what's holding them back.

Where the coachee lacks confidence, I've found that questions which bring out their strengths, personal qualities and other resources are really useful to boost confidence. For example:

- What would people who know you say your strengths are?

- Which other ones can you add to this?

- Which strengths have you used so far in pursuit of your goal?

- Which other personal and external resources do you have that you can use here?

Other questions which build confidence include:

- When are you at your most confident?
- Tell me about a time when you weren't feeling confident about something initially, but later felt more confident about it?
- What happened to increase that confidence level?
- What can you take from this to help you with this goal?

Sensitively challenging any limiting beliefs will help too, as I discussed in Chapter 4. In addition, proactively finding out what they believe about their goal right at the start of the process can uncover obstacles that you can begin exploring and finding solutions for.

Returning to rapport, what do we already know about it?

Rapport occurs in our relationships in varying degrees and is generally dependent upon the level of connection or "sameness" we share. We may share the same:

- Values
- Culture
- Religion
- Hobbies

- Work habits

- Motivation style

- Sense of humour

- Type or place of work

- Tastes in fashion or food

- Place of birth

Personally, I always love to hear a Geordie accent. It makes me feel like I'm back home, even though I now live in the middle of England!

We already know that when we coach someone, we need to build trust, which comes from a connection or things we have in common. However, we don't want to start a coaching conversation talking about ourselves and sharing our family history in order to engender "know-like-trust." And even if we share common ground from working in the same organisation as our coachee, it doesn't mean we will naturally have rapport.

So what can we rely on to generate rapport if it's not naturally there?

Let's look at what's in your rapport-building toolkit.

When we meet a coachee for the first time, we need to build rapport and trust as quickly as possible. It needs to feel authentic, not forced, so we can engage the coachee and maintain that engagement throughout the coaching process.

There are three things that we already have in our coaching toolkit for building rapport:

- Our coaching mindset, including belief in the coachee and unconditional positive regard
- Our ability to actively listen
- Our skilled questioning, which shows how well we are listening and value what the coachee has shared

One of the clearest ways we can demonstrate how well we're listening is not only to ask pertinent questions, but to use some of the coachee's language when we do so. This is part of the mirroring and matching process, and includes matching body language, gestures, speed and tone of voice.

I personally find matching a coachee's language feels more natural than trying to match their body language. Coachees like to feel listened to (don't we all!), and we evidence this by using their words and phrases in our questions and when we summarise what we've heard.

Here's an example scenario:

> Following initial greetings at the start of the third session...

Coach:	So how have you got on with your actions from our last coaching session?
Coachee:	[Smiling] I'm happy to say I've been quite productive! I've now got a useful system for getting my jobs done most days, and I can go home at the end of the day, feeling both satisfied with my day, and ready to actually relax in the evening.
Coach:	[Smiling with the coachee] That's great! And along with being quite productive, with a useful system for getting your jobs done most days, what else have you achieved?
Coachee:	[Smile widening] Well, believe it or not, given my reluctance to do this

when we talked about it in the last session, I've also been delegating some of the tasks that I like doing myself to some of my team members.

In the above example, if the coach had said, "And along with being *productive, each day*, what else have you achieved?", the coachee could spot this and think, "I was quite productive, but not always, and it wasn't *each day*." At this point the coachee might believe the coach isn't listening or fully respecting their view of events.

When I did my initial coach training, I learned about the "Dance of Rapport," where the level of rapport between you and the coachee is in constant flux. Sometimes the coachee leads and you follow, sometimes you're in complete sync with each other, and at other times you're in a "leading" position where you can offer more challenge to overcome obstacles and encourage growth.

What do these look like in practice?

When the Coachee is Leading

The coachee tends to lead this dance, albeit subconsciously, at the start of a coaching relationship. It can also occur at other times, such as when you haven't worked together in a while and rapport needs to be re-established.

Coachees often arrive at the start of a coaching programme wondering or waiting to see what their coach will do. The coach on the other hand is watching and listening for clues about how the coachee is showing up – how they're feeling about the session and what thoughts they have about their goal or current situation.

As the coach asks their initial questions, they start listening and observing the coachee, picking up on key words and phrases that the coachee ascribes to their thoughts. The coach also notices the body language, tone of voice, gestures and other "steps" in the dance that the coachee is leading with.

When the Coach is Matching

Now it's the coach's turn to follow, also known as "pacing" the coachee or, using the analogy of the dance of rapport, the coach is keeping in step with the coachee. They do so by matching the coachee *subtly*. I emphasise that last word, since the aim is to be *close* but not exact.

In summary, matching (or mirroring) can be with:

- Gestures
- Facial expressions
- Tone and pitch of voice
- Body language/position
- Words and phrases

Whichever method(s) you choose, it has to feel authentic. If you don't feel comfortable crossing your legs to match your coachee's position, don't do it! Both you and the coachee will be distracted in the session by you shifting around in your seat trying to get comfortable. Even small movements of discomfort will be picked up by the coachee, consciously if not subconsciously, which can impact flow.

If you're coaching someone online and can see them on video, you'll have some visual clues, but may rely more on verbal and audible ones. If you're coaching on the phone, you only have what you hear (and sometimes don't hear) to mirror or match. Therefore great listening and appropriate questioning will be crucial to maintaining rapport and coachee engagement.

Whilst on the subject of coaching someone online (or on the phone), engagement can be reduced or lost during the session due to distractions in the coachee's environment. So as part of the initial contracting process, check in with the coachee whether they're in a confidential environment, whether they're alone, and if they have any potential audible distractions turned off.

Of course we can't plan for every eventuality, but recognising and minimising potential distractions will go a long way towards this.

To summarise this section, at the start of a coaching session the dance of rapport begins with the coachee setting the pace and the coach matching their steps, until they are in sync. Once this is evident and the conversation is flowing and easy, there's a level of trust where the coach can ask more probing questions. Even if they feel a little uncomfortable, they will be more likely to work hard to find an answer.

Before I conclude this chapter I'll let you in on a little secret...

I kept getting stuck whilst writing this! Unsurprisingly, it's the chapter that took the longest time to write.

I had *so* many ideas and thoughts about it, I kept getting confused and found myself asking, "How can I simplify this?", or "Do I really need that bit?" or "What am I trying to say here?" or "What do I need to leave in? What can I take out?"

Talk about getting stuck writing about being stuck!

In the words of Steve Mehr, "You get what you focus on. So focus on what you want."

Whilst recollecting my experiences of coaching, training new coaches and supervising other coaches, I was doing a lot of focusing on being stuck.

This leads me to ask the following questions:

What are our coachees focusing on when they get stuck in a session?

How do we help them change their focus to something useful and developmental?

And do we create the right environment of trust to facilitate the coachee's journey through and beyond being stuck?

Summary

- We can address the concept of being stuck both proactively at the start of the coaching relationship, and in the moment during coaching sessions when it arises.

- Being stuck is actually a positive part of the coaching process. It represents an opportunity to find new solutions to problems, and increase the coachee's resourcefulness to solve similar problems in the future.

- As coaches we need to embrace these stuck moments, confidently armed with a range of strategies that will help our coachees find the best ways forward.

- Our ability to build a good level of rapport is key to positively navigating a stuck state. We can do this in different ways, but particularly through our coaching mindset, active listening, and appropriate questioning and summarising using the coachee's language.

Actions

1. Decide if you're going to discuss "getting stuck" during the contracting stage with a coachee.

It may depend on the coachee and what previous coaching experience they've already had. How will you raise the subject so the coachee sees it as something positive?

2. Make a list of all the possible ways you could respond to "I don't know."

Try them out in your coaching and make sure they sound authentically you. With further experience, you may evolve to having a "go to" phrase you can use in different moments when a coachee becomes stuck.

3. Check your rapport-building toolkit.

Which skills and strategies do you regularly use in order to build and maintain rapport?

What else can you add to this toolkit to keep the coachee engaged during the session?

Part 4: Engaging in Next Steps

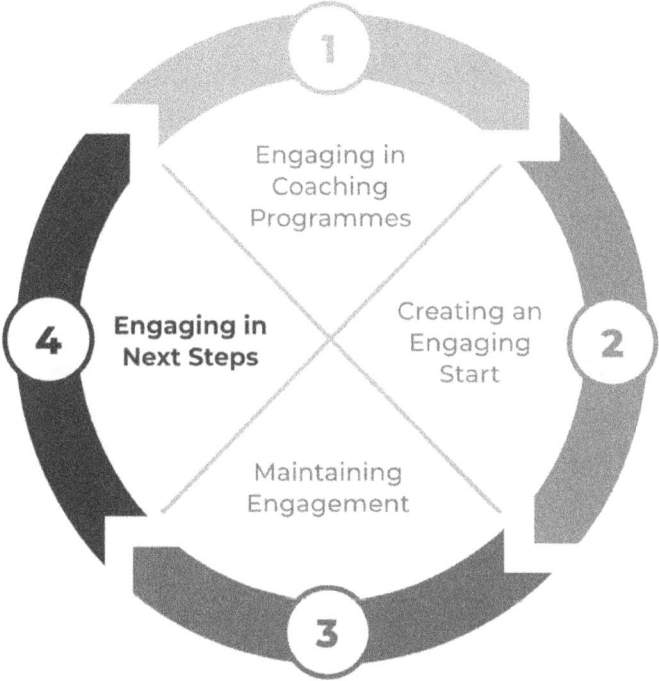

Engaging in Coaching Programmes

Creating an Engaging Start

Maintaining Engagement

Engaging in Next Steps

1
2
3
4

What's the best ending to a coaching session you've ever had? What made it so? What about the best conclusion to a coaching programme?

And what about the worst end to a coaching session or programme of sessions that you've experienced?

A strong finish is just as important as a strong start, if not more so.

Imagine you're watching a film. You're fully engaged, curious and excited to know how the various threads in the story will come together. You want to know how the hero will triumph over their various challenges, only to have the film end abruptly before the conclusion, leaving you frustrated and disappointed.

Or, you're the hero of the film, fully immersed and giving it your all. You have overcome various obstacles and gained new powers as a result, only to realise you're not quite sure what to do with them. As a result, they aren't used to their full potential.

Whether you're the coach or coachee, a weak ending to a session results in feelings of dissatisfaction and untapped opportunities to maximise learning.

In this final part of the Coaching Engagement Model™, I'll start in Chapter 6 by exploring how we can create strong finishes, boost session outcomes and facilitate our coachee's continued engagement in their learning beyond the sessions.

Then, in Chapter 7, I'll explore what we do at the end of our coaching sessions and programmes to ensure that we continue to learn and develop as coaches. This will include exploring a variety of models and approaches for continuous learning, and strategies to maximise this learning to continually engage our current and future clients and coachees.

Help your
coachees see the
wider impact of
coaching beyond
their goals

Chapter 6
Creating Strong Endings

Where do your coaching skills and confidence lie when it comes to concluding your coaching sessions?

How motivated and engaged are your coachees when they leave the session?

And on a scale of 1 to 10, where 10 is the clearest finish to a session and the coachee is most engaged in their next steps, what score would you give yourself?

I remember when I started coaching, I was so focused on having a great start and being able to think of questions in the main part, that my endings were a little lacklustre by comparison. I'd probably have given myself a 5/10. Now, I'm a confident 9/10 (believing there's always room for improvement), and will share what I've found are effective and engaging ways to conclude a coaching session below.

Although it's perhaps not this...

Scenario 1

> The coaching session has been progressing well. You've discussed their progress since the previous session, identified the focus for this session and spent the rest of the time on this topic.
>
> Then suddenly, you notice your time is up and as you attempt to quickly wrap things up, the coachee exclaims:
>
> "Oh, is that the time?! I really need to go. I have an appointment I can't be late for." [Starts to gather their belongings.] "Thanks for today, it was useful." [Gets up to go.] " See you next time. Bye!" [And abruptly leaves.]

Or this...

Scenario 2

> You've explored options and solutions with the coachee and are wrapping up the session.

Coach:	"So we've got a couple of minutes left. What's your action from today's session?"
Coachee:	"Erm… I might try one of those ideas that we've just talked about."
Coach:	"Which one?"
Coachee:	"I might try being more assertive with my team."
Coach:	"Great. So we need to book in our next session. How about the same time in two weeks?"
Coachee:	"I think that works. I'll check after my next meeting and get back to you."

Do either of these sound familiar?

Scenario 2 has a slightly better ending than 1. But you're still left with the frustrated feeling that the conversation has dropped off at the end of the coaching session, having no definite conclusion or clear next steps.

So before we start looking at what constitutes a strong finish, we need to ensure there's time for one.

When I've run out of time, it's usually been for one of two reasons. Either I didn't have access to a clock that I could easily glance at without it being obvious I was checking the time, so I guessed the time, rather than looking at my watch. Or, I was aware of the time, but the coachee was working through something significant and I didn't want to interrupt them.

Our coaching training teaches us to provide our coachees with time and space for them to reflect and share their thinking. So this is ultimately about good time management of the session, and there are a couple of simple strategies you can use to help with this.

1. Let the coachee know that part of your job is to keep an eye on the time.

   This means they can put all of their energy and focus into exploring and working towards their goal.

   You won't need to say this every time, or with every coachee, but it's important that they're aware you're doing this. If you can, sit where you can see a clock, ideally somewhere behind the coachee, so you can subtly check the time.

Respecting your coachee's time and yours will also safeguard your time for reflection afterwards, and being on time for your next activity or session.

2. Carry out mid-session check-ins, which let the coachee know where they are within the timeframe of the session.

   One way you could check-in is to ask, "So we're about half-way through the session, and thinking about your goal for today, where are you now?" and then follow that with, "And where would you like to go next?" or "What would be the best use of the rest of this session?"

   These check-ins are a useful pause point to help the coachee reflect on the session so far, summarise any new learning, ideas or conclusions, and decide what to focus on next. This maintains momentum towards their session goal and helps you focus your next questions.

A good extension to this idea is to let the coachee know how long there is left, as you enter the wrap-up and start asking your wrap-up questions. This, again, can be subtle.

For example:

- "As we move into the last ten minutes…what's been most relevant about today's session?"

- "In the five minutes we have left…what will be your key takeaways?"

Now that we've created the time, how best do we use it? In the next section, I'll share what I believe to be the three core elements to a strong session conclusion.

Before we look at
what makes
a strong finish,
we need to
ensure there's
time for one

A strong conclusion to a coaching session involves:

1. Reviewing outcomes against the session goal

2. Capturing the coachee's key learning and new insights

3. Identifying engaging and motivating next steps

Let's explore how we can make the most of each of these key elements.

1. Reviewing Outcomes Against the Session Goal

For this we return to the contracting piece that took place at the start of the coaching session, and which I explored in Chapter 3.

What did the coachee want to achieve in this session?

I've been surprised at times when I've *assumed* the coachee has achieved their outcome, based on what they've shared in the session. But then I've followed the process and asked a review question, only to find the coachee hasn't achieved their goal. This is a prime example of trusting the process and not making assumptions.

Suffice to say, one of my key learnings in my coaching journey has been that coachees don't share *everything* relevant and important that they're thinking when responding to your questions. They filter out some thoughts and reveal others. For example:

- They might share what they think you want to hear, as they build rapport and trust, or gain more confidence.

- They may need more time to reflect on a question, and have been doing this as the session has progressed.

- They may just give you a summary of their thinking, perhaps only sharing one side of an internal argument.

And when you ask a review question you can uncover some key thinking that you would otherwise have missed.

So which review questions could you ask?

Here are a few ideas:

- "Your goal at the start of today's session was (re-state the coachee's goal phrase or description). How far has this been achieved?"

- "As you reflect back on what you wanted to get from our session today, how would you summarise the outcome?"

- "If 10 out of 10 represented achieving today's goal, what's your score?"

- "How much closer are you to achieving your overall goal for this coaching programme?"

This last one is great for looking at the wider picture if there's a larger goal they're working towards. It can also provide a focus for what to work on next.

These questions are a useful introduction to the conclusion of your coaching session, and lead nicely into specifically identifying their key learning points.

Never make assumptions about what a coachee has gained from a coaching session

2. Capturing the Coachee's Key Learning and New Insights

This is a key feature of the wrap-up process for three reasons:

1. Sometimes the coachee isn't aware of what they've gained in the session, and these questions raise their attention to that.

2. It promotes depth of learning when adding further questions and resources that align with the coachee's preferred learning styles.

3. It draws attention to the value of coaching, particularly for coachees who may have been sceptical about it at the start.

This last point also reduces the risk of a coachee leaving a session thinking, "I'm not quite sure if I've learnt anything new today?" Of course that may be true! But hopefully we'll have facilitated some sort of movement towards their goal at a minimum.

Which Questions Capture Learning?

Here are some examples:

- "As we wrap up today's session, what have been the key moments?"

- "What has today revealed about you/your goal?"

- "What's your main takeaway from today?"

- "What have you learned about yourself?"

- "Which word or phrase sums up today's session?"

- "What else?"

- "If you knew at the start of the session what you know now, what might you have said to yourself at the start?"

I think "what else?" is such an underused coaching question.

In my own coaching sessions, when asked a question which prompts an idea, it's often given rise to another idea which I'm keen to share. Not all coachees will volunteer additional ideas. So it's important that we offer them the opportunity to do so through asking, "what else?" and repeating it (or similar) until they have nothing else to add.

Imagine this scenario...

The coachee has been promoted in their organisation and the coaching has been about how to make this a smooth transition for their team, as well as themselves. In this second session, coach and coachee have explored delegation of some of the coachee's roles before they move on, providing team members with useful experience of *their* new roles. The coachee has struggled with this.

Coach: "What have you learned about yourself in this session?"

Coachee: "That I need to let go, and trust my team to do their jobs."

Coach: "What else have you learned?

Coachee: "That I *do* actually believe they're capable. They're a great team; really talented and successful... but..." [Trails off and looks back at the coach.]

Coach   "But?"

Coachee: "… I've been too controlling lately. I'm really happy about the promotion, but I guess part of me doesn't want to leave them."

Coach: "As you think about this, what else have you learned about yourself today?"

Coachee: "Hmm… That I enjoy building a team! As I think about it now, part of me is looking forward to building and working with my new team."

Which Tools or Resources Capture Learning?

Questions alone aren't the only means of eliciting new insights, learning and progress.

Visual and practical resources work well too, particularly with coachees who process and embed new ideas when they have something to look at or physically interact with.

Here are a couple of examples:

Image Cards

As a visual learner, I enjoy using image cards to prompt or inspire my own reflective thinking. I've also found that many of my coachees have enjoyed these too.

In Chapter 3, I shared how I use image cards as a check-in, and the same cards can also be used when concluding your session.

Questions or guidance to accompany the cards include:

- Choose a card or image that represents a key learning point for today.

- Which image summarises today's session?

- Choose an image that reflects your next steps.

Which other questions could you ask?

Also invite them to share the reasons for their choices and, depending on time, ask follow-up questions to deepen their learning. Remember to maintain your curiosity.

Nested Dolls

Originally known as *Matryoshka* or Russian Dolls, the idea of these wooden dolls of decreasing size has expanded to include animal themes, and can come ready decorated or you can paint your own.

Here's an example of a set of these being used in a coaching session.

Imagine this scenario...

> During one coaching wrap-up discussion, a coachee was sharing how she felt things were more aligned and organised. She made reference to other people, and I followed this up with, "Who are the key players in your plan for next month?"
>
> When she shared who they were and the different roles they would play, I asked if I could introduce a resource to explore this further. She agreed and I brought out a set of animal-themed nested dolls, setting them out individually in front of her. I followed this with, "As you think about your plans, who do these represent?"
>
> She lined them up into two small and separate groups, with another doll a little distance from the group, which represented herself. The coachee talked about how she would be "flitting between the two groups," then paused as if re-

evaluating the situation. I remained silent, curious to see what would happen next.

Initial Positions

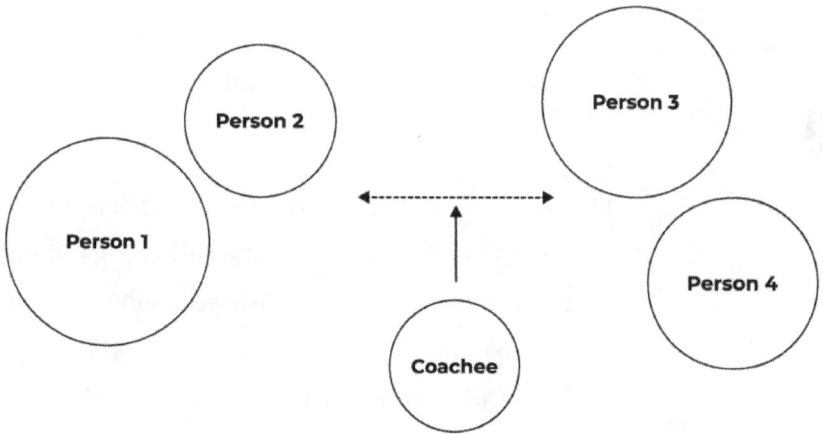

The arrangement went through two further iterations, before settling on two groups, with herself in the smaller one. She explained that in the new staffing arrangement she'd be spending most of her time in the smaller group, trusting that the other team would not need to be overseen as much as she'd anticipated.

Final Positions

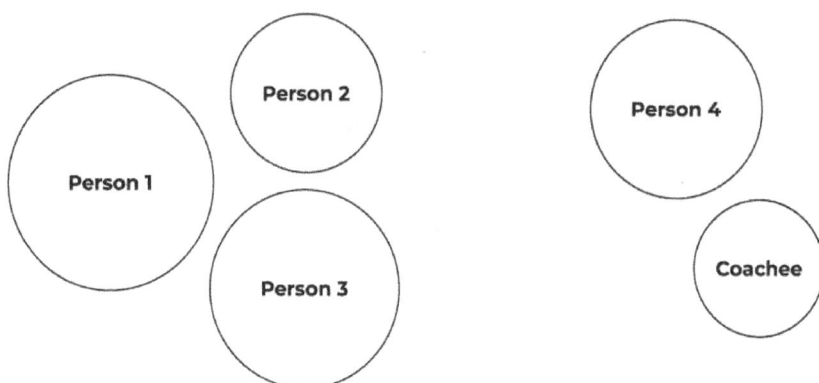

As she surveyed the arrangement now in front of her, she felt more confident and certain that her plans for the new overall team would work well for all concerned, particularly the stakeholders, and would align well with the organisation's wider vision.

Nested dolls are just one example of physical resources that can be used to represent different elements of a coachee's story, such as characters or ideas. Others include buttons, Lego, pebbles or beads. When working online or by phone, you can ask the coachee to use whatever is at hand!

3. Identifying Engaging and Motivating Next Steps

When following a coaching model such as GROW, you will use the "wrap-up" section to filter through the different options that the coachee has come up with, exploring the merits of each, before choosing the best ones and identifying next steps. You may also ask the coachee about any related support they need.

Questions might include:

- Which options appeal to you?
- Which option would make the biggest difference?
- What will your first step be after leaving today's session?
- What support, if any, do you need?

Tailoring Actions to Maximize Engagement

When identifying next steps, there's a real opportunity to tap into how a coachee learns best and how they're motivated to keep going when facing challenges.

I've found different ways of doing this.

Tapping Into Their Preferred Motivation Style

Charvet (2019) explores different motivation styles, including "towards" and "away from." People can be motivated towards a goal or end point, or away from staying where they are. One style of motivation is pulling them forward, the other is pushing them away from a current situation. Both involve movement in a direction that coaching can support.

To identify a coachee's preferred style, you can ask, "What will achieving this give you (or do for you)?" when the coachee has identified their goal at the start of a coaching programme.

Those motivated *towards* their goal tend to talk about what they'll have or gain. They will seem energised by their goal, and like to be reminded about it, although may have trouble identifying problems or what needs to be avoided.

Those motivated *away from* their situation will talk about their problems and what they want to avoid, eliminate or solve. They will be more energised by deadlines and pressure, although may have difficulty maintaining focus on tasks because they get distracted when they see a problem to fix.

Just as we use the language of the coachee to inform our questions, summaries and observations, we can use information about their motivation preferences to ask questions that will support their motivation beyond the session with next step tasks.

Questions to support *towards* motivation:

- "If we were to break the task into smaller steps, what would they be?"

- "Which problems might you encounter with this task?"

- "How will you recognise them? And how will you overcome them?"

- "What will your priorities be, as you focus on your next steps?"

- "How will you reward yourself when you've achieved this task?"

- "Once you've completed that task, how much closer will you be to achieving your overall goal?"

Questions to support *away from* motivation:

- "What will be a good deadline for this task?"

- "Which future problems will completing this task solve?"

- "How will it do this?"

- "What will happen if you don't complete this task?"

- "How will you avoid potential distractions?"

Two things to note:

1. We can exhibit *both* motivation styles around a particular goal. If you hear language from the coachee which evidences towards and away from motivation, employ questions from both styles when identifying and clarifying your coachee's next steps.

2. The preferred motivation style you identify is contextual. It will be linked to their goal, and not necessarily their motivation style for all goals or lifestyle choices.

Post-it Notes

I've found post-it notes are a great visual and practical tool for supporting the decision-making process when a coachee is considering their options. For example:

- As the coachee shares the options they are considering, I write each one on a separate post-it note, making sure I use the coachee's words, and place them in front of us.

You could ask the coachee to write them out; I just find doing it for them in this case gives them more time to think of other options.

- I then invite the coachee to order the post-its according to a criteria of their choice; for example, from easiest to hardest, or most to least beneficial to their goal.

- Looking at the top 1-2 options, I ask the coachee to share the benefits of each option, writing these on separate post-its, and placing these next to the relevant option.

- We then explore the impact of these benefits and I ask the coachee to choose an option. This is followed by identifying specific actions, any support and relevant timescales.

There are several websites that offer digital "post-it" tools, when working online with a coachee. Or you can invite the coachee to use their own post-its, if they have them, or use blank postcards or bits of paper.

The physical act of moving the post-its around really suits coachees who prefer that practical approach as they process their options. It also works well for those who prefer to focus their attention elsewhere than eye-to-eye contact.

"Permission to..." Cards

Referred to in Chapter 3, these cards are brilliant for encouraging engagement beyond the coaching session.

What will they give themselves permission to feel, do, be, achieve between coaching sessions, or when completing their tasks?

Of course you don't need the cards to ask this question; they are just a prompt. Nevertheless, they will suit those who like to learn and remember things visually, or prefer to have something else to focus on.

A Final Thought About Embedding Learning and Engaging in Next Steps

I've worked with coachees who are naturally reflective and will ask themselves questions and verbalise their responses with their coach, giving you a better indication of the learning they are taking from the session.

I've also worked with coachees who like to plan, or are all about taking action, or like to carry out research and reading around their goal area.

If in doubt, ask them what kind of activities work best to embed new learning and maintain their motivation and engagement in their goal.

Concluding a Programme of Sessions

So far this chapter has mainly focused on ways to ensure quality endings to individual coaching sessions. Most of these ideas can be adapted when you come to the final session in a programme of sessions (sometimes called an "exit session"), although there are some differences.

Firstly, the last session will involve more time reviewing the goal(s), reflecting on the outcomes of the programme, summarising learning, and identifying next steps.

Secondly, capturing learning and progress over the whole programme may involve using tools such as the Wheel of Life (or Work). There are many adaptations to this, as it's such a versatile resource. If you've used it at the start of a programme of sessions, you'll have scores for the areas you've identified around the wheel. By repeating this exercise at the end of the programme, you will hopefully show increases in scores around the wheel, particularly in the areas you've been working on.

Reviewing learning and identifying next steps may involve completion of another tool – a personal or professional development plan (PDP). I've completed these with coachees during our final session, or they've completed the PDP after the session and sent me a copy. This usually happens when working in businesses or organisations, but not always.

There are different versions of PDPs, the simplest one includes:

- The goal or goals and associated deadlines
- Actions to achieve the goal
- Resources to support goal achievement

Often an organisation will have its own version of this that you need to follow, but if you have the flexibility to do so, co-create one with your coachee in a way that works best for them. This may be the design of it, creating more bespoke headings, or something else.

Thirdly, the questions you usually ask to capture learning at the end of each session can be adapted to review the programme as a whole:

- "As we wrap up this coaching programme, what have been the key moments?"

- "What have you learned about yourself?"

- "How will you take this learning forward? Where will you apply it?"

- "What things have surprised you that you weren't expecting?"

Ultimately, you want to leave this programme of sessions with the coachee feeling they've achieved *more* than they'd hoped for. The questions above have the potential to show the wider impact your coaching has had, and the work your coachee has done on themselves. This provides a sense of fulfilment for you both, and increases the potential for more work with that organisation or coachee, or a referral to someone else.

Self-Reflective Questions:

How do you conclude coaching programmes?

How do you feel afterwards?

In the next chapter, we'll delve into this further as we explore how you reflect on your practice and maintain your own levels of engagement.

Summary

- We need to ensure there's time for a strong finish, provide coachees with the opportunity to share their learning and progress, and identify next steps.

- Continue your non-judgemental curiosity through into the wrap-up process, and avoid making assumptions about your coachee's learning or takeaways.

- Questions alone aren't the only way to capture learning. Visual aids and other resources provide useful additions to your coaching toolkit.

- Knowing your coachee's preferred motivation style for their goal adds useful information you can use when identifying how they choose and complete their next steps.

Actions

1. Reflect on how you manage the time in your coaching sessions.

   Identify what else you can do to ensure you have time for a good quality wrap-up.

2. Identify questions you can ask to measure progress.

   Do this for both the session goal and their overall goal where appropriate.

3. Expand your coaching toolkit to include visual and other resources to use in the wrap-up process.

   Alternatively, consider how any existing resources you use in the main part of the session can be utilised in its conclusion.

4. Find out how your coachee is motivated in respect to their goal.

   Experiment with different questions that address one or both types of motivation. Observe the coachee's reaction and adapt where necessary.

Chapter 7
Spicing Up the
Reflection Process

Reflection is an essential part of a coach's ongoing development. It happens both within and beyond our coaching sessions. Schön (1983) refers to these respectively as:

- Reflection *in* action

- Reflection *on* action

Reflecting *in* action is more automatic. We can't help reflecting on our practice as we navigate our way through each coaching session.

This process is fluid and our thoughts are fleeting. They result from what we hear, see and feel in the moment. We're thinking on our feet, adapting our practice accordingly. We think about the impact we're having, what's going well, what isn't, and whether we need to change anything. For example:

- That question went down well.

- I wonder why they were frowning there?

- I could have phrased that question better.

- It seems as if they're avoiding the issue; how can I raise their attention to this? Or should I wait to see if they spot it themselves?

Reflecting *on* action involves setting aside time to consider some aspect of our practice, a coaching session, or series of sessions for example. How much time we spend on this depends on circumstances, the importance we place on this practice, and how much we enjoy doing it!

The University of Cambridge defines reflective practice as, "the ability to reflect on one's actions so as to engage in a process of continuous learning." The fact that there's no requirement to do this in a particular way allows for much flexibility in *how* we carry out those reflections. In fact, we can choose when and where we do it too.

In this chapter, I will share a variety of ways to reflect **on** your practice, using the wealth of evidence we have.

The suggestions will range from those we do on our own to group reflective practice activities.

The aim of this chapter is for you to choose the models or activities you prefer and which keep you engaged and motivated in your ongoing development. Alternatively, you could use the ideas to create your own!

I will then conclude the chapter coming full circle, as I explore how we can maximise the evidence we collect from coachees to engage more clients and continue to grow our coaching practices.

Why reflect in the first place?

I believe this is important for two reasons:

1. As coaches, we facilitate the practice of reflection with our coachees, increasing their self-awareness, enabling goal achievement, and promoting their ongoing development. So why shouldn't we do this for ourselves?

2. With coaching still being a relatively fledgling profession, it's important that we demonstrate a consistent approach and commitment to our development as coaches, through evaluating our practice against recognised standards (from

organisations such as International Coach Federation, the European Mentoring and Coaching Council, and the Association for Coaching).

When we don't reflect…

- We miss out on opportunities for growth and impact.

- We risk making the same mistakes; perhaps even attributing errors to something about the coachee.

- Our lack of commitment to reflective practice could "leak" into our coaching sessions, evidenced for example through a lack of depth of questioning resulting in superficial progress for the coachee.

- We can be under the illusion that our practice is fine, and nothing can be improved; this does a disservice to our clients.

- We risk bad habits developing, reducing our impact as a coach, thereby leading to fewer referrals or repeat business.

- We also risk imparting a confusing or incorrect message about the coaching profession, making it harder to promote coaching and its true benefits (e.g. when we include mentoring in our sessions, but still maintain that we've been coaching).

But what if we're not doing much coaching?

I've heard this several times from coaches new to the profession and those who have other income streams or roles in their organisation.

In all cases, your formal reflection practices (e.g. supervision) need to be proportionate to the amount of coaching you do. If you belong to a coaching organisation, check their recommendations.

Otherwise, if your plan is to grow your coaching practice:

1. Adopt reflective practices that are appropriate for the other work you do, so that when your coaching increases, you'll already be employing reflective habits which you can continue with or adapt for your coaching reflections.

2. Engage in supervision, or some form of peer support, to look at the type of coach you are, what your coaching message is, and how you can attract more clients.

When we
don't reflect,
we miss out
on opportunities
for growth and
impact

How to Reflect: Models, Tools and Strategies

Do you have a particular reflective practice model that you prefer to use?

Is it one of the more formally recognised models or one you've created yourself?

Most coaches I've spoken to regularly reflect soon after their coaching sessions using either informal or short formal models, such as:

- Making notes once their coachee has left.
- Using a short formal model, such as "The 3 Whats"
    - What happened?
    - So what?
    - Now what?
- Using a set of favourite questions they've drawn from previously used formal models.

And do you always reflect on your own, or does your reflective practice include sharing thoughts on your practice with others?

Reflective practice books provide useful detail on the more formal methods. As a comparison, I've shared below some of my favourite informal methods, including a few I've created myself. I've separated them into reflective practices we can do on our own or with others.

Individual Reflective Practice Ideas

Self-Generated Question Models

I'd like to share two models; a simple one that reflects some of my favourite questions, and one that's based on using our senses.

Simple Question Model

- What am I drawn to as I reflect on that coaching session?

- What does this tell me about my practice in that session?

- What does that mean for future sessions?

As you can see, this is similar to the 3 Whats, which was my inspiration for this short, sharp reflection. Admittedly, it often leads to additional questions, which peel away more of the layers of my practice leading to new insights or future actions.

Which questions would you choose for a simple model?

Sensory Model

- What's my overall feeling from this session?

    - Why do I feel this way?

    - What might be contributing to this feeling?

    - What's my gut feeling?

    - What can I take away from this?

- What did I notice that's important?

    - If I was an observer of this session, what would I see?

    - How am I responding to the coachee?

    - What did I notice about body language in that session?

    - What *didn't* I notice that's important?

- What did I hear?

    - How did I use or manage silences?

    - Which questions provoked the biggest response?

    - What feedback did the coachee provide (consciously or subconsciously)?

    - What was my internal dialogue during and just after the session?

Resources (e.g. Image Cards or Sets)

I've mentioned image cards a few times in this book already, so you can tell they're a favourite of mine due to their versatility. Previously the focus was on using them with your coachees; now it's your turn!

Focusing on your practice, answer the questions below using either your own image cards or one of the image sets you can download here:

https://go.theleadershipcoachingacademy.com/bookresources

- Which image is most like your practice right now?
- If you were to make some changes to that image to represent potential changes in your practice, what would it look like now?
- What, if anything, is missing from this image?

- How could you enhance the image to enhance your practice?

What other questions would you ask yourself?

And my final question for this section:

As you reflect on your learning from this book, which image are you drawn to, and why?

Artistic / Creative Reflections

Do you like to draw while you reflect?

Here are questions to use as a starting point:

- If I represented the last coaching session as a journey, what would that look like?
- How would I represent the programme of sessions I've just completed?
- What are the key points of interest on this journey?
- What can I say about them?
- What can I learn from them?
- How do they impact my future practice?

If drawing is not your thing, what about modelling, or creating something using lego or other building blocks?

Which reflective practice questions would go well with this type of learning?

Reflective Walks

I've often found that walking after a coaching session is the perfect way to process what has happened, and to critically reflect on my practice. I'll either use questions that pop into my head, and ensure there's a progressive structure to the process, or I'll use one of the formal models I can recall.

See Chapter 5 for more on the benefits of using the outdoors to promote creative thought, and below for "Group Walks".

You can build metaphors into your reflective walks too! The environment is a great source of inspiration for metaphors, which leads us nicely into the next resource.

Metaphors

In the book, *Metaphors We Live By*, Lakoff and Johnson define metaphor as, "understanding and experiencing one kind of thing in terms of another." For example:

- That coaching session went by like a whirlwind.

- I kept thinking he was going around in circles, and nothing I asked seemed to move him forward.

- The ideas and enthusiasm of my coachee today felt like there were sparks going off all around us.

Do you naturally find yourself creating metaphors when you reflect and try to make sense of things that have happened?

Perhaps in your next reflection, ask yourself: "If I were to think of a metaphor for my last coaching session, what would it be?" or "What could I compare my last coaching session to?"

Of course you can also widen your reflections to your overall practice, and look for patterns (or metaphors) there.

Knowing my creative preferences, my supervisor once asked me, "If your coaching practice was a musical instrument, what would it be and why?"

I loved this question! It might have something to do with the fact I'm also musical, but I don't think it would have mattered. She could have asked me:

- If my practice was a chocolate bar, which would it be and why?

- Or if it was a piece of furniture… and so on.

I made some notes on this session afterwards, an excerpt of which I've included in the next section, "Journaling". I really enjoyed that session as it tapped into my visual and creative learning preferences.

Journaling

Many people I know, particularly coaches, have a journal for recording their thoughts and feelings. The act of writing helps us to process things that have happened; we're filtering, choosing and ordering as we write.

There are lots of lovely journals or notebooks you can buy now, which can make journaling feel a bit more special.

Journaling can involve anything from a stream of consciousness to following a highly structured model, as long as there's an intention to engage in a process of continuous learning.

Here's an extract from my journal, following a one-to-one supervision session:

In today's supervision session, my supervisor (Carole) asked me a great question:

"If your coaching practice was a musical instrument, what would it be and why?"

I started off thinking of a saxophone, because I love that sound ("Baker Street" anyone?), but then I couldn't easily link it to my coaching practice.

I then thought of a piano. The white keys were 'me' and the black keys were "the coachee." The black keys are sharps and flats. The sharps are coachee insights and the flats are obstacles or things that don't resonate for the coachee.

Being the white keys, I act as a platform or support for the coachee's growth and development.

The image is changing... I'm now imagining a duet scene... my coachee and I are playing a duet. We are co-creating the tune or piece of music, bringing into the composition all of our resources, mindset, attitudes and behaviours in that moment. Any 'wrong notes' can either indicate opportunities for learning, with no judgement, or we're out of rapport.

Carole offered some follow-up questions to take this learning forward beyond our session. These included:

1. How often and what would I practise?

2. What else might I bring into the composition?

3. How would I know what impact the practice is having?

4. What does my best session (duet) look, sound, feel like?

I'm drawn initially to the last question.

My best session ...

- Has good flow and energy.

- Has good pace, but with slower, quieter periods too, as we maintain the "duet of rapport."

- It has lively and fun moments where ideas are generated.

- It has a natural and authentic feel; nothing is forced and I don't have to think hard about which note to play next (i.e. which question to ask).

I've heard the question, "What does (x) look, feel and sound like?" a number of times, but it held so much more depth off the back of creating the duet metaphor.

It's prompted me to think again about my "coaching state" as I prepare for future sessions. I'm sitting at the piano waiting for the coachee to arrive. We don't have the music in front of us yet; that will be determined by the coachee. I am confident that I'll be able to "sight-read" the piece of music once we start, and as I listen to the coachee's part, my fingers will find the right notes, and my brain will think of the best questions...

Self-Reflective Question:

What kind of reflections do you capture, if you journal?

Verbal Reflections

Not everyone enjoys writing things down. Plus, with our busy schedules, sometimes you need a quick alternative. This is where verbal reflections come in.

You capture your thoughts on some sort of recording device whilst they're fresh in your mind. You can listen back to them later and where appropriate, record additional insights or conclusions. There is also software now that will transcribe your audio recordings; just search for 'transcribing audio to text' and you'll be provided with a range of options to choose from.

"Juicy" Questions

These are questions that you may not hear very often.

As you will notice, from some of my favourites below, they tend to have more than one part to them, encouraging depth and breadth to your thinking.

1. If your coaching practice was represented as a shape, which would it be and why?

2. Is your coaching more transactional or transformational at the moment? What's your learning from this?

3. What differences do you notice coaching in an organisation compared with coaching private clients? What conclusions can you draw from this?

4. How do you manage coachees who seem less engaged? What's your evidence for lack of engagement?

5. What are your preferred coaching tools? If you were to make a case for other ones, what would they be and why?

6. Choose three different coachees that you've worked with. Put yourself in their shoes and describe how they may have experienced working with you. What, if any, patterns emerge?

7. Are you drawn to particular coachees? If so, why, and what does that tell you?

8. Which coaching sessions do you enjoy the most? What is it about them that makes them enjoyable? What learning can you take from this?

9. What's the biggest insight or learning from your practice to date? What led to it, and how are things different now as a result?

10. What do you tend to shy away from in your coaching practice? What are the pros and cons of this?

Which of these do you like best?

What are your top three?

Paired or Group Reflective Practice Ideas

Co-coaching

This is also known as peer coaching, and it has lots of potential for reflective practice straight afterwards, using whichever model or strategy you prefer.

For example, following each coaching session the "coach" shares their own observations drawing any early conclusions if they wish. Then the "coachee" offers feedback, including how it felt to be coached. The conversation and feedback may go back and forwards several times, before the "coach" offers their final thoughts and any next steps. Then the roles are reversed, and the process repeated.

Group Walks

As well as the aforementioned benefits of walking while you're thinking, the subject of these group walks could either involve:

- The group as a whole reflecting on a particular aspect of their practice, such as contracting or managing distractions, learning from each other's experiences, and identifying any changes to their practice.

- Or, individual members bringing their own topic, and having a set amount of time to reflect, with prompt questions from the rest of the group. Make sure that there's sufficient time for everyone to participate and the group size isn't too large; six is a good size, but I'd avoid groups larger than eight, unless you plan on pairing up or dividing into smaller groups.

Coaching Communities

One of the main reasons I set up my Supervision Plus Membership Group for coaches was to generate a coaching community, where coaches could continue their development through asking questions, sharing challenges and successes, and feeling vulnerable in a safe, supportive environment.

Feedback from members points to the live sessions being the most useful. In this forum, members enjoy being able to talk through their issues, benefiting from thought-provoking questions which promote mobility in their practice. Most of all, they like knowing that they're not alone!

If you enjoy working through reflective practice topics with other coaches, find a buddy or community that inspires and motivates you to regularly reflect and learn.

Using Resources / Images

Previously in this chapter I shared some questions to accompany image cards or sets, plus ideas for resources, for individual reflection.

With a group of coaches, this process is enhanced, as there will be no shortage of follow-up questions you can ask each other with your "coaching hats" on! You may just need to put a cap on the time each person is offered, to ensure everyone gets a turn.

Supervision

Although I've shared a variety of models and tools for reflecting on your practice, *supervision* is crucial for your ongoing coach development. I've experienced one-to-one and group supervision over the years, and find both to be equally valuable.

With one-to-one supervision you have the whole time to yourself, and can share things you may not do in a group setting.

With group supervision, you have the opportunity to bring a topic or case study for reflection, but can also learn from other members of the group, and the topics they bring to the session.

In my coaches membership group, members will sometimes say at the end, "Although I didn't have a topic to bring today, I have learnt *so* much from listening to everyone else!" or, "I love being asked questions by different people; you get lots of different perspectives with group supervision."

When I named this chapter, I wanted to draw attention to the ways in which we can add interest, variety and creativity to the reflective practice process. With this in mind, take a look at the questions below. How would you answer them?

Self-Reflective Questions:

Having reviewed the different reflective practice ideas, what's the perfect combination for you right now?

Which ones appeal most to your preferred method of learning?

Which will challenge and develop you further?

Using Evidence to Grow Your Coaching Practice

If I was to ask you, "When it comes to your coaching, how do you know you've done a good job?"

What would your answer be?

Most responses from coaches I've spoken to or worked with have centred around external feedback:

- I've received a glowing testimonial!

- My coachee has achieved their goal and more.

- The coachees leave the session happy and with a clear plan.

- I've had great feedback from the coachee/the coachee's line manager.

- The coachee said they've been able to open up and be really honest with me, which has meant achieving results faster than they thought.

I find this statistic unsurprising. Coaches often choose this profession from a desire to help and develop others. We see evidence of this in coaches' marketing messages and materials, including websites, on digital profiles and in social media posts. There's a strong 'people' focus, so we will inevitably seek feedback from relevant external sources.

Other responses to that question have stemmed from internal evidence, where success is measured against the coach's internal set of criteria of what "good" looks like.

- It felt really good. I listened well and my questions were flowing naturally and easily.

- In a good session, I'm present throughout and don't get distracted by my own thoughts.

- At the moment, a good session is where I don't start mentoring when I get stuck for a question!

- I measure my practice against core competencies from the coaching organisation I'm a member of.

There's no right or wrong here. When reflecting on our practice, we're using evidence; whether that's from internal or external sources, or both.

I believe that by incorporating *both* elements we widen the scope of information we can use to regularly improve our practice. Using a breadth of evidence avoids our development being based on assumptions.

This next section looks at different ways to gather and use that external evidence to promote your coaching, develop new interest, and increase engagement in your services. Success breeds success!

So, how do you currently gather evidence from your coachees?

There are two ways to do this, direct and indirect.

The direct approach is to *ask* them for feedback. I've come across several coaches who don't do this, either because it feels self-serving and uncomfortable, or because they're not sure how to without coming across as, "Aren't I great! Please tell me what you love about working with me!"

Here are my thoughts on this:

- Let your coachees know that part of your own ongoing development is to regularly gain feedback from clients, and would they mind completing a short questionnaire. Have digital and paper versions to suit different preferences. Agree a date by which they'll return it.

    I also often ask for permission to send them a nudge if I've not heard anything from them, acknowledging that other things can get in the way. No-one has said "no"… so far!

- Help those who've offered to send feedback, but despite their positive intention, it doesn't happen.

  You can do this by routinely capturing positive feedback from a coachee in a session, then offer to share it with them so they can add to or amend it. It's much easier to edit something that's already there than feel as if you're starting from scratch.

- Create a case study by giving the coachee a structure to tell their "story." For example:

  - Where they were before they started working with you

  - What challenges you helped them overcome

  - The outcomes they gained by the end of the programme

  - Any additional learning, such as new insights about themselves

- If they've given you some written feedback, ask if they could replicate this on social media, or ask if they mind you putting this on your website or other promotional material.

The indirect approach includes using unsolicited "feedback," such as gifts or unprompted comments and testimonials on social media, and using patterns of evidence, such as data on a theme from a number of sessions.

Perhaps the two most successful uses of data are:

1. The return on investment or return on expectations that a client has received. This may take the form of an individual case study, but several case studies or sets of data will provide statistical evidence of your coaching impact in general.

2. The language coachees use when they talk about their outcomes, and what it's been like to work with you. The words and phrases a coachee uses are important to capture because they'll resonate with other potential clients with similar challenges or issues.

If you're an internal coach in an organisation, and aren't marketing your services in the same way as an independent coach might (as described above), it's still important to share how coaching in your organisation helps people in order to maintain engagement in your coaching offer and continue to facilitate success.

So coming full circle, let's look back at Chapter 1 where I talked about how your coaching message needs to speak to the coachee's problem or issue, and the solution they are seeking.

Considering the evidence you are gathering from your coachees:

- What changes, if any, could you make to your message?

- How might you adapt the language you use?

- Who could you ask for a testimonial?

- Whose success story could be turned into a case study, with their permission?

- What data do you have that you could collate and share as part of your marketing message?

And what else could you do?

Summary

- This chapter has shared a variety of reflective practice models and strategies, including suggestions to create your own. It's important that you choose one(s) that will motivate and inspire you to keep learning and engaging with your own ongoing development.

- When we don't reflect, we miss out on opportunities to be better coaches, serve and engage more clients, and make a positive impact

- Collecting evidence from our coachees in the form of direct and indirect feedback will help build confidence, increase credibility, and create the best language to describe how you help people.

Actions

1. Identify some models and strategies that work well for maximising your reflective practice.

   Which will you use most often?

   Which will you use for more complex events where you need to go deeper with your thinking?

2. Create your own model to use on a regular basis.

    This can come about from using a range of different models and creating a hybrid model. Whilst doing this, use what you know about how you learn best, and weave this into your bespoke model.

3. Find a coaching community that will motivate and support your ongoing development.

    Coaching can be a very solitary profession, and coaching communities that value collaboration over competition often provide that lovely combination of support, positive challenge, accountability and networking opportunities.

4. Identify a coach supervisor if you haven't already got one.

    This supports accountability, expands your learning opportunities, and adds weight to your credibility as a coach.

5. Create a strategy to gather coachee feedback.

    Be bold and find a way to ask your coachees for feedback, if you're not doing it already. Build this into set times in your programmes, so it becomes common practice.

Don't be shy about sharing good feedback; it will help you to build your "social proof" and generate new interest.

Conclusion

An engaged coach and coachee is the most important part of the coaching process. The more engagement there is, the greater the chance for success.

In this book, I've introduced you to the 4-Part Coaching Engagement Model™, which details the range of opportunities we have to help build and maintain engagement throughout the coaching process and beyond.

I've shared the importance of creating engagement before coaching even begins, the benefits of being suitably prepared and the process of creating a clear start. I've explored how *you*, as the coach, can avoid disrupting engagement, and how you can respond to a coachee who's stuck.

I've also detailed different ways to capture learning and deliver effective conclusions to sessions, and shared creative strategies for maximising your own engagement within your reflections and learning.

Here are some key takeaways from each part of the book:

Part 1
Successful engagement from the start involves clear communication and managing the coachee's expectations so that they know what they're buying into. Therefore, it's important to make sure that there's time for a pre-coaching conversation where any misunderstandings can be addressed and you can begin the process of how you'll work together.

Part 2
Ensure that both coach and coachee build in time to prepare, and that the coachee has some ideas on how to prepare for each session effectively. When starting your coaching sessions, ensure that you're both clear on what the session will be about and the outcome you're working towards through a contracting process.

Part 3
It can be helpful to design and wear your "coaching coat," or create something similar which will give you confidence and keep your focus on the coachee to keep you in flow and engaged. Sometimes, the

coachee will inadvertently interrupt flow when they become stuck. Identify a strategy you can use in response, such as questions that generate "possibility thinking" for the coachee.

Part 4

There are a variety of ways to wrap up a coaching session, but always make sure that there's time for a wrap-up. And never assume you know what a coachee has gained from a session. Instead, ask them. They may surprise you!

And finally, there are a number of different and creative ways you can reflect on and learn from your own practice. If you're currently using one method or model for reflection, or you only reflect on your own, try one of the other approaches mentioned in the last chapter to create variety and new ways to learn.

If you feel there's a point in your coaching process that isn't working as it should, or you're looking to refresh an aspect of your practice, you can dip into the relevant part of the model for ideas, strategies or solutions.

If you're at the start of your journey as a coach, you now have a model to build or increase engagement in your practice, supported by a range of ideas from which you can choose. Don't feel like you have to use them all! Pick what works best for you.

See this book as a resource of practical ideas which build engagement in order to maximise coaching outcomes.

Let's face it, there's a lot to think about when running a coaching practice, and anything that can make the experience run more smoothly and create successful outcomes is a welcome resource.

Ultimately, I'm guessing that your aim is to have a successful coaching practice that positively impacts individuals and organisations.

You've got the skills. You know the potential that coaching offers for ongoing personal and professional development. Now it's about making it the best experience possible for your coachees!

You can access and download resources that support the themes in this book by visiting https://go.theleadershipcoachingacademy.com/bookr esources or by scanning the QR code below.

Here you can also find my coaching, coach training programmes and supervision.

Wishing you all the best with your coaching practices. You've got this!

References

A. Gilbert and K. Whittleworth, *The OSCAR Coaching Model: Simplifying Workplace Coaching*, 1st edn., Worth Consulting Ltd., 2009.

B. Bassot, *The Reflective Journal*, Palgrave Macmillan, 2013.

G. Lakoff and M. Johnson, *Metaphors We Live By*, The University of Chicago Press, 2003.

J. Canfield and P. Chee, *Coaching for Breakthrough Success: Proven Techniques for Making Impossible Dreams Possible*, McGraw-Hill Education, 2013.

J. Whiltmore, *Coaching for Performance: Growing Human Potential and Purpose - The Principles and Practice of Coaching and Leadership*, 4th edn., Nicholas Brealey Publishing, 2009.

S. Gilligan and R. Dilts, *The Hero's Journey: A Voyage of Self-Discovery*, Crown House Publishing Ltd, 2016.

S. R. Charvet, *Words That Change Minds: The 14 Patterns for Mastering the Language of Influence*, Bloomanity LLC, 2019.

W. Thomas and A. Smith, *Coaching Solutions: Practical Ways to Improve Performance in Education*, London, Network Continuum Education, 2009.

Coaching Organisations:

Association for Coaching. *Association for Coaching*, https://www.associationforcoaching.com/, (accessed 5 August 2024).

European Mentoring and Coaching Council, *EMCC Global*, https://emccglobal.org/, (accessed 5 August 2024).

International Coaching Federation, *International Coaching Federation (ICF)*, https://coachingfederation.org/, (accessed 5 August 2024).